Living Questions
Teacher's Resource Book

SUE HASTED AND GEOFF TEECE

Stanley Thornes (Publishers) Ltd

First published in 1993 by:
Stanley Thornes (Publishers) Ltd
Ellenborough House
Wellington Street
CHELTENHAM GL50 1YW

Reprinted in 1993, 1994 and 1996

A catalogue record for this book is available from the British Library.
ISBN 0 7487 16262

Designed and stylised by Claire Brodmann
Printed and bound in Great Britain

Acknowledgements

We should like to acknowledge the part played in the development of these materials by Garth Read. Garth was Director of the Regional RE Centre (Midlands) from 1980 to 1988 and during that time was the driving force behind the Westhill Project. He has since moved back to Queensland where he continues to play a major role in curriculum development in RE.

The basic structure of *Living Questions* comes from Garth's work and we have developed it into its present form. We thank Garth for his support and inspiration.

The authors and publisher acknowledge the kind permission of copyright holders to reproduce the following material:

The *Guardian* for extracts from two articles: 'Parents on the Front Line', Madeleine Bunting, 17 September 1991 on p. 34; and 'Habit for Life' by Julie Johnson, Young EGO, 15 October 1991 on p.59; Pan Books for extract on p.45 from *The Hitchhikers Guide to the Galaxy*, Douglas Adams.

CONTENTS

INTRODUCTION

Living Questions is designed to be used, primarily, with Key Stage 3 pupils. It forms part of a larger set of materials known as the Westhill Project.

This resource book is designed to be flexible. Teachers may choose, in the light of knowledge about their own pupils, which topics and which activity sheets to use with any particular group within the 11-14 range.

The resource has two components. (1) A pupils' book dealing with seven Life Themes, each with four topics on double page spreads. (2) A teacher's book with notes on the themes, and a set of photocopiable activity sheets for class use.

Pupil activity sheets

For each Life Theme in the pupils' book there are nine photocopiable pupil activity sheets contained in the teacher's book. Some activity sheets may be used by adopting a whole class approach whilst others demand smaller group work; some may be suitable only for the more able pupils. They are designed to follow up, broaden and deepen the questions that are posed in the text of the pupils' book.

The systems approach

Classroom materials, in the form of books and photographs, which adopt the *systems approach* are already published and the theoretical underpinning of this approach can be found in *How do I teach RE?*, pp 40-41. Within a *systems approach* to religious education, the aim is to help pupils explore an aspect of a traditional belief system in order to develop an understanding of that system and how it relates to various aspects of our shared human experience. Within this approach only one tradition is the focus of attention at any one time. In other words, the aim is to help pupils develop a better understanding of what it means to be, for instance, a Christian or a Jew or a Muslim.

The life theme approach

The approach adopted in *Living Questions* is the *life theme approach*. A full account of this approach to teaching RE can be found in *How do I teach RE?* pp 41-45. Again, by way of a brief summary, we may suggest that within a *life theme approach* to religious education the aim is to help pupils explore an aspect of shared human experience in order to

develop an understanding of that experience and the 'fundamental' or 'ultimate' questions it raises. These kinds of questions are those which, if answered at all, must be answered by an expression of belief. Questions such as 'Is there a God?', 'Who am I?', 'What is life for?', 'Why did the world begin?' and 'Where do people go when they die?' are obvious examples. However, the task of religious education is not simply to help pupils grapple with these fundamental questions which arise out of our shared human experience of the world. It is also concerned to involve the pupils in considering more than one religious or non-religious faith response to such experiences and the questions they evoke.

For example, the first section in the pupils' book takes the Natural World as the overriding Life Theme. The introductory topic, *What are we doing on Earth?* challenges pupils to consider both scientific and religious ways of describing the universe. Questions about the origin and existence of the universe are posed and explored through both scientific explanations and several creation stories from the religious traditions. Having introduced the theme, this section then goes on to explore it more widely in the subsequent three topics. The topics contain questions for pupil reflection and research. Teachers may use these in any way they see fit: as discussion questions or as ways of breaking up the topic over a number of lessons.

Following on from the Natural World are six other themes, namely: Celebrations, Relationships, Stages of life, Lifestyles, Rules and Suffering. These themes are chosen because they represent aspects of our shared human experience that pose for us and our pupils these fundamental questions about life. They also provide a rich context for exploring religious responses to such questions.

The structure of the pupil book and themes and topics contained therein are as follows:

The natural world
1 What are we doing on Earth?
2 Are there miracles and mysteries?
3 Chance or destiny?
4 Is the world full of wonders?

Celebrations
1 What do we celebrate?
2 How do we celebrate?
3 Why do we celebrate?
4 Who do we celebrate with?

Relationships

1 Are we unique?
2 Alone or together?
3 Why do conflicts happen?
4 Breaking up or making up?

Stages of life

1 What is life for?
2 What shall we do next?
3 What's the right thing to do?
4 Is the time right?

Lifestyles

1 What is 'the good life'?
2 Here and now or hereafter?
3 What improves the quality of life?
4 What threatens the good life?

Rules

1 Why do we have rules?
2 What do the rules really mean?
3 Are there any rules which never change?
4 What happens to rule breakers?

Suffering

1 What is suffering?
2 Has suffering a place?
3 Can suffering be a means to an end?
4 How can we cope with suffering?

Theme teaching and the agreed syllabus

The question of the appropriateness of teaching RE through a thematic approach has been an important feature of debates about the subject in recent years. There are those from within both the religious and political spheres of life who have spoken out against a type of theme teaching that, in their view, trivialises religions and blurs distinctions between them. The authors of *Living Questions* would agree that there are some approaches to theme teaching that do create these problems. Themes like sacred books, leaders, pilgrimages and initiation rites can, if badly handled, lead to a blurring of distinctions and misrepresentations of the faiths being studied. For example, it is nonsense to pretend that there is anything within Islam that approximates to the Christian practice of baptism. The calling of the *adhan* in the young Muslim baby's ear is not an initiation ceremony in the same category as baptism. Indeed it is not an initiation ceremony at all. The baby doesn't have to become a Muslim, he/she is born one!

Similarly it is potentially confusing to place the Gita of Hinduism alongside the Qur'an. They are both sacred scriptures but they do not carry the same level of authority, for example, in their respective traditions. Here lies the potential for misunderstanding and misrepresentation. One has to approach such themes very subtly if the pitfalls are to be avoided.

However, whilst it is sound advice to warn against the potential problems of unthinking approaches to themes within religions, it is our view that theme teaching of the kind presented in *Living Questions* is an important part of RE teaching. In fact the questions and issues which we explore in these materials lie, we believe, at the heart of RE and the human quest for meaning. This view is reinforced by the chairman of the National Curriculum Council, David Pascal. Talking about spiritual development he says,

> Questions about the origins of the universe - the purpose of life - the nature of proof - the uniqueness of humanity - the possibility of certainty - the meaning of truth - these are often explored in RE lessons. But how often do teachers of other subjects take time to discuss such issues with pupils, often leaving them with an exaggerated view of the infallibility of science and of the inadequacy of religion and philosophy as valid ways of viewing experience and existence.
>
> Schools must be sensitive - and indeed usually are - to the fact that for a number of children, spiritual development is linked inextricably with their religion. Despite the important distinctions between religions, we share common values - not only with those of other faiths, but with the majority in our society who subscribe to no faith at all.

The Life Themes approach, as we have indicated above, is an ideal vehicle for helping pupils explore these common concerns of the human quest for meaning. Many of the recently published Agreed Syllabuses reflect this approach in some sections of their programmes of study.

The National Curriculum Council's Analysis of SACRE reports informs us that up to April 1992, 43 local authorities had produced, or were in the process of producing, a new agreed syllabus for religious education. This figure has increased since then, particularly in the light of the legislation arising from the White Paper which calls for LEAs to review their syllabus, if they have not already done so.

Even though RE is, and has always been, locally determined, there are a number of common elements evident in these new syllabuses. Most, if not all of them, take into account the structures of the orders for the core and foundation subjects. There are, of course, a number of different models. Some syllabuses resemble the Geography model whilst others model themselves more along the lines of History, for example.

However, what is common is a general consensus as to what the subject is about. Within the models of attainment current in local documents is a view that religious education is about pupils coming to understand the relationship between what people of religious traditions believe and do and the more general and widely shared concerns of humankind's search for meaning and purpose in life. It is not the intention, however, that pupils merely learn about this but that they should also learn from this.

Here are a few examples taken from the programmes of study of recently published Agreed Syllabuses. The subject matter of *Living Questions* can help teachers meet these requirements.

LEA Programmes of Study and Living Questions: Some examples

Leicestershire (1992)

Pupils should have the opportunity to:

investigate and respond to stories of creation from different sources, examining the beliefs which underlie them and the contribution that such religious stories make to a sense of human purpose. **(What are we doing on earth?)**;

investigate and reflect upon a variety of awe-inspiring natural phenomena and accounts of miraculous and unexplained events. **(Are there miracles and mysteries?, Chance or destiny?, Is the world full of wonders?)**;

develop their understanding of family and community relationships by comparing family and community life in a variety of settings. **(Alone or together?)**;

consider some examples of the effects of religion on individuals and on society. **(Alone or together?, Why do conflicts happen? Breaking up or making up?)**;

distinguish between ordinary questions and questions of meaning and purpose (ultimate questions) and consider a variety of responses to ultimate questions, including those given in some religious traditions. **(All questions).**

Clwyd (1992)

In the course of their investigation and exploration of religions and life-experiences pupils should be encouraged to identify and discuss a variety of ultimate questions, contemporary concerns and

moral issues. Pupils should see these questions, concerns and issues arising out of everyday experiences as we seek to make sense of both human knowledge and the underlying mysteries of existence. **(All questions).**

Bedfordshire (1992)

Pupils should have the opportunity to:

explore religious rituals and ceremonies associated with important stages in individual and community life **(e.g. bar mitzvah, baptism)**;

understand how religious communities express indentity and affirm beliefs and values through rites of passage;
develop understanding of the concept of commitment in a religious context. **(Stages of Life questions)**;

appreciate how religious and moral principles influence relationships. **(All Relationships questions)**;

explore why religious commitment is important to some people and how it is expressed. **(Relationships, Stages of Life and Life Styles questions)**;

develop positive attitudes towards cultural diversity, gender equality and people with disabilities. **(Alone or together?, Why do conflicts happen? Making up or breaking up?)**;

become aware of various stories of the origins of the world and human life. **(What are we doing on earth?)**;

appreciate that different religious traditions have different ways of understanding the relationship of human beings to the natural world. **(All Natural World questions)**;

be familiar with a variety of attitudes and responses to change, decay and death, and with some religious ideas/beliefs about death and life after death. **(All Suffering questions).**

Hampshire (1992)

Pupils should have the opportunity to:

continue to develop their understanding of their own patterns of belief and values as they relate to the universal issues, questions and experiences in the spiritual and religious life of humankind, including the basic questions posed by the mystery surrounding the existence and purpose of the universe and human life. **(All questions)**;

the basic questions posed by some of the fundemental dilemmas in human life-death, conflict, suffering, evil,etc. **(Stages of life, Relationships, Suffering questions)**;

the sense some people have of the 'transcendent' and of an underlying pattern of meaning and purpose in life. **(All questions)**;

the human quest for a sense of order, peace and harmony with self, others and the environment. **(All questions)**.

Cleveland (1992)

Pupils should have the opportunity to:

consider, in greater detail, questions about life, identity and destiny, e.g.Who am I, Why am I here?, How should I live?, How do I know what is true or good?;

further consider experiences which raise questions of meaning and purpose **(of confusion, suffering, death, wonder, joy)**;

study some response to these questions and dilemmas from different religious traditions as shown through doctrines and beliefs (e.g. free will, love, compassion, forgiveness, justice and mercy); reflect on religious and scientific views about the earth and human responsibility for it. **(All questions)**.

For further reading

Teachers who wish to follow up some of the areas discussed in this introduction are advised to consult the following books:

How do I teach RE? by G Read, J Rudge, G Teece, R Howarth (Stanley Thornes, second edition 1992)

Attainment in RE: A Handbook for Teachers from Regional RE Centre (Midlands), 1989

Assessing, Recording and Reporting RE: A Handbook for Teachers from Regional RE Centre (Midlands), 1991.

THE NATURAL WORLD

TEACHING NOTES

The pupils' book theme

Using the scientific method to explore and explain the world is relatively new in human history. Explaining natural phenomena in spiritual and/or supernatural terms has a much longer history. Most people are aware of a continuing, if not growing, tension between these two ways of understanding the natural world. This tension may spring from ways in which both of these approaches have produced constructive as well as destructive attitudes and achievements in terms of human well-being. Another reason is a lack of understanding about the roles that both science and religion play in explaining reality.

The first topic seeks to challenge pupils to see science as essentially concerned with what can be known and demonstrated, and religion as concerned with a different kind of explanation which involves mystery and faith.

Work done in the second topic seeks to help pupils identify different and similar characteristics in feats of magic, illusion and deception and in accounts of totally mysterious happenings which seem to defy any logical or scientific explanations. Accounts of this kind are drawn from both traditional scriptures and contemporary events.

The third topic draws attention to the wide range of beliefs that people hold about the ways in which fate, faith and the stars influence human life. With this age group the emphasis should be on encouraging them to collect and collate as many as possible of the arguments for and against such beliefs. They should also be encouraged to suspend their judgements until they have considered and reflected on the force of the different arguments.

The mood and emphasis of the fourth topic is rather different. It challenges pupils to formulate and express some of their own beliefs and values in respect to the natural world by seeking to identify what, for them, are the great wonders of the natural world. Increased understanding of the role of beliefs and values is likely to occur when these lists are put alongside other well-established claims about the wonders of of the world. These lists can also be compared with the examples in the text about the 'wonders of the world' which have been built by human effort.

The Activity sheets

The first three activity sheets accompany *What are we doing on Earth?*

1 This activity sheet provides an opportunity for students to think about the place of humanity in the universe by looking forward into the future, rather than back towards creation. Evolution can be seen as a process culminating in the arrival of humans as the 'crown of creation'. But is this really the case? What is, or should be, our role?

2 It would be worth reading some creation stories aloud, and discussing some of the questions raised on this sheet before handing it out. An extension activity for the more able is to make up their own creation story, explaining all the aspects of existence that most puzzle us.

3 The aim of this activity sheet is to bring out clearly the role of belief in our interpretations of the world. Factual evidence can be adduced to back up a particular hypothesis or belief about the way the world works. This is the case with scientific pictures of the universe, just as it is with religious pictures of the universe.

4 This activity sheet provides some fun to go with *Are there miracles and mysteries?* You will need three dice to demonstrate the trick, if you are doing it with a small group. This should help to bring out the distinction between illusion, whether deliberate or an accident of perception, and genuinely unexplained mystery.

5 The story of Hagar tells of a miracle, as does the story about Jesus in *Are there miracles and mysteries?* The activity sheet allows interrogation of both stories, which should focus on the concept of 'a miracle' and the elements which make up miracles: special powers and unusual happenings which seem to contradict nature, the link between these and the power of God, the relationship of those who are agents of the miracle, or to whom it happens, with God, and the role of faith. If it is possible to talk about such happenings with members of the faith traditions, students may become aware that there are a number of responses to reports of miracles, which vary even within the same tradition.

6 The question of fate goes to the heart of the debate about free will explored in *Chance or destiny?* This activity sheet, with a few possible responses to aid discussion, should fuel a lively debate. To ensure a good mix within small groups, it can be useful to ask the class initially to divide into two groups: those who believe in 'fate' and those who do not. Those who do will usually have stories to tell, so ask them to tell them in

order to clear the way for the discussion, which can otherwise be sidetracked. Then make sure that each small group contains students from both divisions.

7 This sheet also accompanies *Chance or destiny?* If we are free, we must also be accountable for our actions: on one level, to society, and on another, to the Creator; this equation is arguably made, in one way or another, by all world religions. Looking at responsibility is therefore another way of looking at free will. It also leads towards a consideration of human responses to those who have made the wrong choices (if choices they are). The question of rules and responses to rule breakers comes up in another form in the section on Rules.

8 This balloon debate is to follow up on *Is the world full of wonders?* and can be done individually if need be. Remember to decide on the religious book or books and the extra item to be carried before starting. Obviously, the aim is to bring out the reasons why students would choose to keep one item rather than another, and the beliefs behind those reasons. It also asks what, if anything, is important about human achievements.

9 This activity sheet is another aid to discussion of the natural wonders of the universe. Some students may not be prepared to admit to amazement of any kind; if so, ask them to contribute by noting down why they *don't* find each item their classmates choose amazing. Task 6 can be done for individual homework or left out if the discussion threatens to take the whole session. Again, the aim is to bring out the beliefs behind the students' feelings about aspects of nature.

Evolution

Where are we going?

Imagine it is the year 30,000 – yes, 30,000! The evolution of the planet Earth has moved on. Think about what has happened in all that time. Which species have survived, and which died out? Are humans still around? Have people changed at all? (Are *you* a human?) We have included one or two ideas to start you thinking.

1 Draw, or describe, the forms of life to be found in the year 30,000 and say why you think these have survived, and others have died out. What is life like now?

> In the late twentieth century it was estimated that the human population of world, then five billion, would double by the twenty-second century.

> By the year 2000, people knew of one-and-a-half million species of animals and 300,000 plant species. Five or ten million species were thought to exist. At that time, human activity meant that one species per day was being lost. Of the animal species, insects outnumbered all others.

> Two-thirds of the Earth's surface is covered by water. In the oceans live mammals such as dolphins and whales, whose intelligence has been compared with that of humans. They have no need of clothes and shelters, farming or industry.

> Dinosaurs dominated the planet for 80 million years, then suddenly died out. Humans evolved over a tiny fraction of that time.

Creation stories

Making a story that explains things is a very basic human activity. We do it all the time. Why do you think this is so? Are some ways of explaining things better than others? If so, why?

 **1 Choose a creation story from one of the major world religions. Read it carefully.**

2 Make a list of the things the story explains. For instance, the story might explain:
- **Where night and day came from**
- **Where the first people came from**
- **Where the first animals and plants came from**
- **Other facts about the universe or human life.**

3 Who is the most powerful being in the story? Can you describe the kind of power they have? Do they ask anything of the first humans?

4 Is there anything your chosen story doesn't explain? If you can think of anything, write it here:

5 What do you believe about the existence of the Earth and the universe? Where did it all come from? Or has it always existed?

Beliefs and evidence

Look at this statement:

'UFOs are vehicles for alien visitors to Earth.'

There is evidence to back up this statement:

- many people say they have seen and taken photos of UFOs
- many such sightings cannot be explained easily
- there are billions of suns in the universe, and so there are probably lots of planets on which there is life.

People have many different ways of explaining the natural world, and it is not always clear that there is a 'right' way. Sometimes it is possible to show what is true; at other times, it comes down to what you *believe* to be true.

When we argue about our different explanations, one thing we usually do is give evidence to support our beliefs: we say *why* we think a particular explanation is true. For example, I can say that chickens come out of eggs, and show you a chick hatching from an egg to prove it.

People who object to the statement say that:

- those who see UFOs are mad or misguided, and their photos are fakes or of other objects
- UFO sightings can be explained in many more simple ways
- no other stars are near enough to Earth for space travel to be possible by any known means.

In both lists of 'evidence', we are talking about beliefs: about how we *interpret* our experience of the world.

 1 Choose one of the statements below, or make up your own. Make a list of evidence for and against it . (Even if you agree with it strongly, you will find it useful to think about what someone who doesn't agree might say.)

God created the universe and all that is in it.

The universe is an accident.

There is a purpose for humankind's existence on Earth.

There is no purpose to life on Earth.

2 Now go through your 'evidence' and underline any statements that are really beliefs, and which cannot be proved.

Magic

Try this magic trick. You will need three dice.

Give your victims the three dice and have them tumble them once, and then stack them up on top of each other. Ask them to add all the numbers that are hidden - the ones you *can't* see. They can pick up the dice to look, but they must not show you.

While they are counting, tell them that you know the answer because you have magic X Ray eyes. To prove it, you will write it down, and when they have finished counting they will see that you have already predicted their answer.

How to do it? Well, the total of any two opposite faces of a die is always 7. This means that the three tops and bottoms of the stacked dice in front of you will total 21. You have already seen the top number. You simply take away the top number from 21, and the figure that is left is your answer. For instance, if the top number is a 6, 6 from 21 leaves 15.

This trick is, obviously, a deliberate deception which counts on your knowing more about dice than your victim.

Q **1 Do you know any 'magic' tricks? Describe here one you have particularly enjoyed.**

_____

_____

_____

_____

_____

_____

2 Now write down as many reasons as you can think of why people are amazed by 'magic' tricks.

_____

_____

_____

_____

_____

_____

3 What are the differences between this kind of magic and the kind of magic that is sometimes called 'superstition'?

                    Living Questions Teacher's Resource Book © 1993 Sue Hasted, Geoff Teece

Miracles

Muslims tell the following story about the prophet Ibrahim's second wife, Hagar. The story is re-enacted by all Muslims who make the pilgrimage to Makkah.

Q 1 *Read both this story, and the one in your book about Jesus's healing miracle, very carefully.*

THE STORY OF HAGAR

When Ibrahim and Hagar's son Ismail was very small, Allah ordered Ibrahim to go to Makkah and leave his wife and son there. So they travelled there, but when they arrived they found a very bare and barren-looking mound in a valley. There was no water. Ibrahim felt he must do as he was commanded, so he left Hagar and Ismail with a bag of dates for food and a leather bottle of water to drink.

Hagar was frightened, and she asked Ibrahim whether he was leaving them there of his own free will, or whether it was Allah's command. When she heard it was by Allah's command, she said 'Then he will not let us die'. So Ibrahim left them.

For a long time Hagar waited, praying for help. She fed the baby and ate the dates and drank the water. When there was none left she began to get very thirsty, and the baby started to cry. In desperation she rushed to the top of the nearby hill (later known as Safa), but there was no water there, nor anyone to help her.

So she ran to the top of the other nearby hill, which was later called Marwah. Again there was no water, and nobody in sight. Back and forth she ran, seven times, praying to Allah for help all the while. Suddenly she heard a voice calling her name. There was an angel, pointing at the ground by Ismail's feet. And at that spot a fountain was gushing out of the ground.

Hagar ran down to drink. Then she filled the bottle and began to dig a well. She gave the well the name 'Zamzam'.

Q 2 *What is the 'miracle' in each story? Describe it in your own words.*

3 *Choose one of the stories above, and write down all the questions you would like to ask the characters.*

4 *What does your chosen miracle mean for believers in that particular faith? (You may need to ask a believer to help you find out.)*

Fated

Form a small group. Imagine you are regular travellers on the Thursday bus to the local swimming pool, where you go for lessons.

One of you has an aunt who often 'reads' the tea-leaves left in her cup, and makes predictions about what will happen. This aunt got very agitated yesterday and came round to the house to warn you not to travel on the bus this Thursday. She said she had 'seen' a terrible accident in the tea-leaves involving a bus, and all your friends' names, too.

What will you do? Decide as a group whether you will take notice of Auntie's prediction or not. Note down your decision, and the reasons for it. Does anybody disagree with the majority decision? Why ?

The responses of the people below will start you off.

_____

_____

_____

_____

_____

Predictions have come true before. It's fate – but if you act on it, you can escape harm.

Nothing in science tells us that you can predict certainties. You can only predict what is likely to happen.

I believe that God will take care of me. If I trust in him, I don't need to fear evil superstitions.

My fate is already written. Nothing I can do will change it.

Living Questions Teacher's Resource Book © 1993 Sue Hasted, Geoff Teece

Are we responsible?

Generally, we think of ourselves as responsible for our actions. Or do we?

Did you know that a few hundred years ago in Russia, mentally handicapped people were put in prison for being 'mad'? People thought that they were responsible for their 'madness' and should be punished for it. Ideas about responsibility have changed.

Criminal law is based on the idea that we are responsible for our actions. If we do something bad, we are held to have freely chosen to do it, and we must pay a penalty to society.

1 Read the following case history.

Tom is 18. His mother died when he was three, and he had no brothers or sisters. For a while his father tried to bring him up, but his father had a problem with alcohol. When he drank, the father would lose his temper and then his job, and he would take it out on Tom. After Tom suffered a broken arm, he was taken into care, and lived in a variety of children's homes from the age of eight to 16. He did not do well at school despite a talent for drawing. Tom was unable to hold down one job, and although he has gone on several courses and has a social worker who regularly visits him, he has not found another one and is currently unemployed.

He has spent several short periods in detention for stealing, and is now on trial for robbery with violence. Witnesses have said they saw Tom hit a woman in a shopping mall and steal her handbag. Since he is now an adult he may be sent to prison.

2 Form a small group and discuss whether you think Tom is really reponsible for what he has done, or not. Did he freely choose to behave as he did? Make notes of your reasons why you think one way or the other.

3 If possible, compare notes with another group who decided the opposite from you.

4 Decide on an appropriate way of treating Tom. Should he go to prison for what he did? If not, what course of action would you recommend instead?

The balloon debate

Imagine that you are crossing the ocean in a large hot air balloon, carrying the human artefacts and inventions in the list. They are either unique, like the painting, or they are the only ones left after a disaster has destroyed all other examples of their kind. You are going to start again in an unspoiled, uninhabited land. Your balloon is rather like Noah's Ark without the animals – the new land already has wild plants and animals!

Half way across, your gas supply runs out and you are forced to throw one thing after another into the sea in order to stay aloft and make it to shore.

Each item weighs the same, so don't worry about throwing the heaviest out first. Which item will you keep for the longest? Which is first to go over the side? Why?

We have printed the items in large print so that you can cut them out and stick them down in the order you finally choose. You might like to write your reasons under each one first.

Before you begin, agree on which religious or sacred book or books you will take. These then travel as a package – if one goes out, they all go out! Also, you can add one extra item of your own choice to the list: agree on this one, too.

- Van Gogh's painting *The Sunflowers*

- A bag of corn seed

- A medical kit including a medical textbook

- An anthology of much-loved poetry and prose

- The complete works of Shakespeare

- A powerful computer with lots of software including encyclopaedia and dictionary

- A religious or sacred book (or books):

- The complete laws of your old country

- A collection of tools for every purpose

- A CD player and all the works of your favourite musician

- Paper, pens and pencils, art materials

- Extra item:

Living Questions Teacher's Resource Book © 1993 Sue Hasted, Geoff Teece

Natural wonders

In the book, we look at some of the wonders of the natural world. Which natural wonders make *you* most full of wonder?

Q *1 In the following space, on the left, list in the pencil the five things that you find most amazing about the natural world or the universe in general. You can choose from the ones in the book, make up your own list, or mix the two. On the right, opposite each item, say why you find it amazing.*

2 Pair up with someone else and compare your lists.
- *Which things have you both chosen? Was it for the same reason?*
- *What different things did you each choose? Why?*
- *Look at your right-hand columns by themselves. Are the reasons you both gave roughly the same? What differences are there?*
- *Has looking at your partner's list made you want to change yours in any way? Do so if you want to. You can also each add another item (to make six) and change your reasons if you want to.*

3 Now form a larger group of four or five. Your task is to agree on a list of the five most amazing items, and your reasons for choosing them. Write them down on a separate piece of paper when you have agreed. Pick one spokesperson.

4 Each group's spokesperson reports to the whole class in turn. Someone writes all the items on the blackboard (not the reasons why). The class then votes for the top five items.

5 Now the reasons why people find the top five items amazing are also written up on the board.

6 Your last task is to think of as many questions as you can, based on the list of reasons. For instance, if you had an item which read: 'repeating patterns in nature/ makes us think it is planned' you could make the reason into several questions by putting it as: 'Is nature planned in some way? If so, is it by God? What kind of God would plan nature this way? If it is not by God, why are there patterns? Do the patterns change over time?' - and so on. See how many questions you can think up!

CELEBRATIONS

TEACHING NOTES

The pupils' book theme

The desire and capacity to celebrate is a widespread human experience. Any exploration of what people celebrate and why they celebrate through, for example, major festivals, quickly leads pupils into an awareness of the multiplicity of beliefs and values by which people live. This exploration may also help the pupils to understand something of the role that beliefs and values play in forming individual and community identities.

The topics selected for study in this theme focus on general questions about the nature of celebrations and the reasons people give for joining in particular celebrations. Helping the pupils to understand the complexity of such personal motivations is also part of the intention of this section.

In the primary years, the emphasis is often on the outward and observable features of a variety of religious and secular celebrations. The intention is to help pupils extend their understanding of a range of different types of celebration, and the kinds of activities used to highlight the importance of that which was being celebrated. In this book the concept of celebrations is being expanded and a variety of reasons which people give for celebrating are explored.

The first two topics in this theme explore what and how we celebrate. The first topic helps pupils reflect on the fact that to celebrate something is to mark it out from the ordinary and the mundane. Usually, this is done by engaging in activities which, at least for the participants, are unusual and which often provide opportunities for considerable fun and festivity. However, it is also important for them to recognise that celebrations can be times for solemnity, deep reflection and restraint.

The second topic looks at three different celebrations and helps pupils reflect on how they are celebrated. It is important to get pupils to appreciate the range of moods which may be reflected even within one celebration, for example Ramadan.

The third topic is intended to help pupils identify and reflect upon some of the reasons given for participation in particular celebrations. Examples explored in this topic are: celebrations as simply opportunities for fun and light-hearted festivity; celebrations as times to draw attention to and perhaps win support for particular causes, beliefs and values; celebrations as one-off occasions which may focus on events such the end of a war or

success in a sporting event; and a major religious celebration, Christmas, which has been maintained and developed over a long period of time. Such a celebration provides a powerful means for uniting large numbers of people, often from very diverse backgrounds of nationality, race and culture, in a shared identity, as Christians. This, of course, is true of other major religious traditions. Thus, we draw attention again to the fact that in religious education the central concern in any topic is with the cluster of beliefs and values which are expressed in the practices being studied.

Two important features of this are explored in the third topic. Firstly, everyone who joins in a community celebration like Christmas may not share the set of beliefs and values which inspired it. The celebratory activities reflect key beliefs and forms of spirituality which it is hoped will be adopted or confirmed by those who participate. In other words, celebrations can have the effect of forming beliefs in individuals which were either not present or only latently present before. Secondly, in most cases neither the beliefs nor the celebratory activities remain static. The durability of any celebration and its capacity to involve a large number of people often depends on the extent to which the activities and the beliefs seem to retain a coherence and a relevance to the lives of those who are asked to participate.

The fourth topic in this section can be used to help pupils relate their general understanding of celebration and why people celebrate to their own lives. In particular it is hoped that pupils may have the opportunity to reflect on those celebrations which are important to them, which people they feel it is important to celebrate with, and which beliefs and values are most important to them. Whilst this gets to the heart of what RE is about, it is important to recognise that pupils have the right to keep personal beliefs and values private.

The Activity sheets

1 The first sheet provides a simple introduction to the idea of investigating why we celebrate. Inventing an alternative method of birthday celebration should raise questions about the link between practice and beliefs or values.

2 For this you will need a supply of newspapers and magazines. This activity can be a class project undertaken during work on the theme as a whole. Sorting the celebrations into classes is intentionally difficult. Overlapping clusters, or repeating examples under separate headings, is

allowed. The process of categorisation should be used to bring out the range and variety of reasons for celebrating.

3 A fun exploration of a secular celebration, this activity aims to encourage closer investigation of the values behind a particular celebration.

4 The activity sheet provides brief historical background to the now defunct Empire Day as a means of allowing students to explore the way circumstances and values, and thus celebrations, change over time.

5 The same activity could be done with songs from other faith festivals if the class is predominantly Muslim or Hindu, for example. However, this sheet extends the spread on Christmas as an example of a complex religious and secular celebration. It should help to bring out the background of beliefs and values expressed in such a celebration.

6 An investigation of the paradox within celebrations - they both express or confirm existing belief for some, and serve to form such beliefs for others. The baptism debate focuses on the two poles of this paradox. The subject can be discussed in class, but care should be taken with the follow-on questions, which elicit personal information which students may not be willing to express in public.

7 Celebrations which emphasise restraint rather than indulgence are essential subjects of exploration in any consideration of the subject as a whole. They also provide an opportunity for contrast with the more secular and commercial values that predominate in 'Western' society.

8 This exercise focuses on the groups and communities who celebrate, and highlights the group solidarity affirmed by most celebrations. It can also help students examine their own sense of belonging to particular groups and communities.

9 This project could be limited to one period's discussion or actually be put into practice over a term. It is placed last because it should help to summarise all the points brought out in the work on celebrations and allow students to express them in a variety of ways.

Birthday greetings

 **1 Read all the birthday greetings below.**

Hoping this greeting
Will help to convey
The many warm thoughts
That are with you today –
And hoping you'll know
That when this day has gone,
The thoughts and good wishes
Will keep going on.

Warm Birthday wishes
are coming your way
for all that will
make this
a wonderful day.

Thinking of you

*Have a lovely
leisurely day!*

Ready! Set!
Off you go!
Have fun!
Hope your birthday's
just great
A real winning one.

HAPPY BIRTHDAY

A birthday card
to tell you
That you're always close
in thought
And you're wished
the very nicest things a
birthday ever bought.

*Fun at home
Fun with friends
Lots of fun all day
That's what your own
special birthday
Is sure to bring yourway
Hooray, it's your birthday*

No wish could be
more warmly meant,
No greeting more
sincere...
Have the happiest
birthday
And an even
happier year.
Enjoy Every Moment

*You are loved!
You are special!
Happy Birthday*

2 Make a list of all the reasons you can think of for celebrating a birthday.

3 Birthdays are usually celebrated by holding a party, inviting guests, giving presents and having a special meal. Can you invent a new way of celebrating, taking account of all the reasons to do so?

 Living Questions Teacher's Resource Book © 1993 Sue Hasted, Geoff Teece

Celebrations collage

One way of finding out what a society considers important is to look at the things it chooses to celebrate. You can do the following either individually, or as a class.

'Help me look good for my wedding day'

Pearly King Syd set for Maltese honour

By CHRIS YANDELL

GOSPORT'S Pearly King – who took part in the fiercest convoy battle of World War II – is to be honoured by the Maltese government.

Syd Seymour was a 17-year-old seaman when he helped to escort a fleet of merchant ships from Gibraltar to Malta in 1942.

Only one of the vessels got through – and many accompanying warships were also sunk.

Mr Seymour is to receive a special medal commemorating the 50th anniversary of the subsequent decision to grant Malta the George Cross for withstanding heavy bombing.

Other people awarded the medal are due to collect it from the Maltese High Commission in London.

But Mr Seymour, aged 68, of Bridgemary Road, Gosport, plans to fly to Malta to receive his medal from the island's president.

"It's a great honour and comes as a bit of a surprise after all these years," he said.

Mr Seymour has been awarded the medal for his part in a "make-or-break" convoy which transported food and fuel to Malta, headquarters of the British Mediterranean Fleet.

Ohio was the only merchant vessel which survived constant attacks by German submarines and Italian planes as the ships headed for the besieged island.

The aircraft carrier HMS Eagle was one of several vessels which fell victim to enemy U-boats.

An Italian bomber crashed on Ohio's deck, but heroic efforts by her crew enabled the American-owned tanker to reach Malta's Grand Harbour.

The 10,000 tons of fuel salvaged from the sinking vessel enabled Malta to hold out against further Italian and German air attacks.

SYD SEYMOUR

Today's birthdays

ACTOR Sir Alec Guinness is 79, sprinter Linford Christie is 33 and actress Penelope Keith is 53.

Celebration time

ISLE OF WIGHT: A "Going for gold" conference is to be held on the Isle of Wight to celebrate 25 years of Rotaract clubs.

The multi-district conference, co-ordinated by Rotaract clubs in Hampshire, East Dorset, South Wiltshire and the Isle of Wight, is being held over Easter.

Rotaract is a world-wide organisation under the umbrella of the rotary club, which helps local communities. This year Rotaract are raising money for the Cancer and Leukaemia in Children charity.

Q

1 Collect a number of newspapers and magazines, local and national, and look for any mention or reports of celebrations. There will be some obvious ones, such as weddings, and others that may be less obvious. Don't forget that some celebrations can be solemn and involve restraint, like Remembrance Day. Cut out a short passage or headline or picture to represent each one you find.

2 When watching television or listening to the radio, make a note of any celebrations reported on news or magazine programmes. Use a separate piece of paper for each one.

3 See if you can sort your collection into categories. For instance, you might decide to put weddings, birthdays and funerals all together and separate them from national holidays, and from sports successes. Or you might simply try to divide religious ones from 'secular' (non-religious) ones.

4 Now make a display collage of your cuttings and notes on a large piece of sugar paper, or on the classroom noticeboard.

5 Write a short paragraph explaining what sorts of celebrations you found and how you chose to arrange them, to go with your display.

April fool!

All Fool's Day, on 1 April, has been celebrated for hundreds of years in many parts of Europe and Asia. Its origins are lost, but similar celebrations were held by the Romans, and by the Celts. There is a Hindu festival known as Holi which takes place at about the same time and also involves mischief, such as squirting other people with coloured water and powder.

The day is very popular in Britain and the custom is to play tricks and practical jokes on anyone and everyone before mid-day. In recent times the media have been involved. Once, BBC Radio had a well-known astronomer tell the audience that, because of an unusual alignment of the Earth and Sun, the force of gravity would be varying in some places that day. He then asked the listeners to try jumping up and down and to report any unusual results by phoning in. Lots of people rang to say that they could jump higher than ever before. Some even said they had floated in the air. Right at the end of the programme, after the signature tune, the announcer whispered 'April Fool!'

Another year, BBC Television put out a long documentary film about the spaghetti crop in Italy, showing various kinds of pasta growing on trees...

 **1 Have you ever played an April Fool's Day trick on someone? Describe any tricks you have played, and the results. As a class, share one or two.**

2 What makes a trick or practical joke a good one? Who laughs? Why do they laugh? Does anything come out of the experience for the jokers, or for those who are tricked?

3 Why do you think people might want to play tricks on each other? In a small group, discuss this. Decide whether it has to do with any of the following:

- **Upsetting the normal order (for instance, tricks by children can undermine parents' authority)**
- **Making people see the world with new eyes**
- **Celebrating the spirit of mischief in all people**
- **Making people laugh at themselves and take the world less seriously.**

4 Can you use jokes or tricks to make a particular point? (For instance, you might trick someone who was greedy into missing all their meals on April Fool's Day.) In your group, think up a trick which aims to bring about a change for the better. The trick could be played on an individual, a group of people, or on the world as a whole.

Living Questions Teacher's Resource Book © 1993 Sue Hasted, Geoff Teece

How celebrations change

EMPIRE DAY

Empire Day used to be celebrated by a holiday and picnics on 24 May, which was also Queen Victoria's birthday. Originally, it was started in memory of the help given to Britain by other countries in the Empire during the war with the Dutch settlers in South Africa: the Boer War (1888-1902).

The British Empire began as far back as 1583 with the colonisation of Newfoundland in North America. As the first country to change from farming to industry, Britain was later in a position to conquer large territories such as India by trade, to provide raw materials for factories in Britain. The goods produced were then sold at a profit all over the Empire - a very large captive market. They were also sold back to the people who had provided the raw materials: for example, the Lancashire cotton mills used raw Indian cotton to make cloth which was then exported to India for sale. Winning wars against other European colonising powers such as France and Spain also added to Britain's overseas territories. For a time, Britain was the richest and most powerful nation in the world.

Britain not only exported goods, but also values, because it was generally believed that they were right for everyone, not just for British people. Missionaries took Christianity to the Empire; British soldiers and administrators introduced our military and political systems too.

North America, Canada, Australia and New Zealand, as well as parts of Africa, were settled by British emigrants. But gradually, in the early years of this century, the new countries broke with Britain and gained their independence. After the Second World War, with Britain drained of resources and far less powerful, a free association of former colonies was set up, called the Commonwealth. Today, its members account for roughly one-fifth of the world's land and population. English is still the most used international language.

Q *1 What did the people of Britain have to celebrate on Empire Day?*

2 Why do you think Empire Day is no longer celebrated? Have our beliefs and values changed at all?

3 Can you think of any other celebrations which have changed over time, or died out? Why did they change or die?

Christmas carols

Songs sung at celebrations often reveal the central beliefs and values that are being celebrated.

 1 Read the following verses from Christmas carols.

a See amid the winter's snow,
Born for us on Earth below,
See, the Lamb of God appears,
Promised from eternal years.

Lo, within a manger lies
He who built the starry skies,
He who, throned in height sublime
Sits amid the cherubim*.

· · · ·

Sacred infant, all divine
What a tender love was thine,
Thus to come from highest bliss
Down to such a world as this!

Teach, o teach us, holy Child,
By thy face so meek and mild,
Teach us to resemble thee
In thy sweet humility.

* small angels

b Good Christian men, rejoice
With heart and soul and voice!
Now ye need not fear the grave;
Peace! Peace!
Jesus Christ was born to save;
Calls you one and calls you all
To gain his everlasting hall.
Christ was born to save.

c O holy Child of Bethlehem
Descend to us, we pray;
Cast out our sin, and enter in;
Be born in us today.
We hear the Christmas angels
The great glad tidings tell;
O come to us, abide with us,
Our Lord Immanuel*.

* 'God with us'

d For he is our childhood's pattern;
Day by day like us he grew;
He was little, weak and helpless,
Tears and smiles like us he knew;
And he feeleth for our sadness,
And he shareth in our gladness.

And our eyes at last shall see him
Through his own redeeming love;
For that child so dear and gentle
Is our Lord in Heaven above;
And he leads his children on
To the place where he is gone.

Q 2 Underline all the names given to Jesus in the verses. What do they tell you about Christian beliefs?

3 Write down as many Christian beliefs as you can find expressed in these verses. For example, there is the belief that God was born as a human baby.

4 Now see if you can detect some of the values expressed in the verses. What kind of world do the writers think humans have made: a good one, or a bad one? What do the verses say about sin? What do they say about dying? How do the writers recommend that children should behave?

Living Questions Teacher's Resource Book © 1993 Sue Hasted, Geoff Teece

Celebrations and belief

In the early Christian church of the second century BCE, the ceremony of baptism was not performed for babies as it often is today. In those days baptism was a ritual reserved for people who had spent as much as three years preparing to become Christians. It was a complicated process, and only after undergoing it could the new Christian join in the celebration of the Lord's Supper (Communion, or the Eucharist).

Today, baptism (or sometimes 'christening') is often performed for new babies and focuses on welcoming them into the family of the Church, announcing their names, and sometimes appointing 'godparents' who undertake to help bring them up as Christians.

Because of this change, some Christian denominations have introduced a new service of confirmation for young adults who have decided to become Christians.

Many people who do not attend church regularly still want to have their children baptised. This has led to a debate between Christians about whether they should be allowed to do so.

On one side are those who feel that people who only use the church for social occasions such as weddings, christenings and funerals are not really serious about their faith. They think that the church should concentrate its energy on other things, perhaps on helping the poor and disadvantaged, or on spreading the Christian message to unbelievers. They say that a register office could perform the social celebrations for those who do not otherwise attend church regularly.

On the other side are those who say that it is the job of the church to provide a service for families at points in their lives when they feel the need for one, as they obviously do. In any case, they say, going through a ritual such as baptism can remind people of a faith they once had, or even introduce them to it for the first time. The ceremony itself includes expressions of belief which may help them to form their own beliefs. They may rediscover beliefs they once held, but have since lost. Contact with the church may prompt them to turn to it for help in the future.

Q *1 Where do your own beliefs come from? Were you simply born with them? If not, how were they formed? If you think of youself as a non-believer, or are unsure what you think, have you arrived in this state by reacting to the beliefs of those around you? Think about this on your own.*

2 Can you think of any celebrations or occasions you have attended which affected how you thought about life? These could be religious or non-religious occasions. Note them down, and say why or how they changed you.

Fasting at Ramadan

Often, 'Western' society seems to value having more of everything: more money, more goods, more choice, and so on. It is not often than we celebrate by giving up anything. Many of our celebrations, too, concentrate on more (more food, more presents, more people). The balance is tipped in favour of 'more', rather than 'less'. Looking at one celebration which involves having less could be revealing. Could it have something to tell us about what we may be missing?

Sawm, or fasting, for the month of Ramadan is one of the Five Pillars of Islam. This means that it is one of the five basic rules of practice for all Muslims. During the month of Ramadan, all Muslims are asked to refrain from eating and drinking, and having sex, during the hours of daylight. At night they may do these things, but they are not supposed to make up for lost time by over-indulgence.

Although people go to work and to school as usual, the fast is an occasion for concentrating on things that may be forgotten in normal times. In particular, Muslims are reminded of the following:

- Saying the five regular daily prayers at set times
- Reading the Qur'an
- Living in a way that demonstrates one's submission (*islam*) to God
- Controlling one's own behaviour
- Being concerned for others as well as oneself.

The emphasis is on self-control and devotion to God. Anger, speaking ill of others, indulgence and idleness must be curbed. Extra kindness to others is encouraged, and may be expressed by giving extra money to charity. Many will say more prayers during Ramadan, and read the Qur'an more often: some will go into retreat at the mosque to do so.

For Muslims, the fast of Ramadan is commanded by God in the Qur'an (in *Sura* II. 185, 187), and thus there is no need to ask the reason why one should do it, since the aim of life is to fulfill the will of God. But fasting is also seen as a demonstration of mastery over the self, which may otherwise over-indulge in human desires and lose sight of its true aim.

Q **1 Can you think of any benefits from self-control of the kind emphasised in Ramadan? (If you are a Muslim, are there any benefits of practising self-control that are not mentioned above?)**

2 Imagine that the government has decided to institute a national period of 'giving up' in order to mark, or celebrate, the general wealth of the nation in comparison with many others. What might they ask you to give up? What might they ask you to do instead during that period?

3 Can you think of any other events, causes or ideas that could be celebrated by a period of self-control?

 Living Questions Teacher's Resource Book © 1993 Sue Hasted, Geoff Teece

Who celebrates with me?

 **1** Use the list of celebrations you made while reading the chapter, or brainstorm as many celebrations as you can think of and write them down in the left hand column below:

2 Now take each one and try to decide who actually does the celebrating. Tick against it in the appropriate column (you may have to have to tick the same one in several columns, e.g. Christmas is celebrated by family, friends, and all the communities.)

Name of Celebration	Personal	Family	Friends	Community		
				Local	Religious	National	International
Christmas		✓	✓	✓	✓	✓	✓

3 Now underline in colour the ones that you celebrate personally. Are there any people you celebrate with more often than others? Are there any people you would like to celebrate with more often? What would you like to celebrate with them, and why?

One World Day

Imagine it has been decided that the international community should celebrate One World Day.

Q **1** **Decide what the aims of One World Day should be. What beliefs are being celebrated? What values should be expressed? Remember that celebrations can help create beliefs as well as express ones that already exist.**

2 **Now invent as many ways as you can think of to create the celebration of One World Day. Remember that:**

- **'giving up' can be as important a way of marking an event as 'having more'**
- **people can celebrate as individuals, with family, with friends, or with a number of different communities.**

Resources at your disposal

You have the world's media to help you. Radio and television can provide instant global communication by satellite link, as they do for some sports and political events and charity shows already. Stars and personalities are often only too willing to help with media events of this kind: they give them plenty of exposure, and further their careers!

Each country has a certain amount of money, but you need to think of things people can do for themselves, too, such as holding street parties.

Music can be extremely useful. You could write an anthem, like 'Feed the World/Do they Know it's Christmas?' used in the Ethiopian famine fund-raising campaign in 1986; or you might choose an existing song, as 'Nessun Dorma' was chosen for the football World Cup in 1990.

Art and design can help too. What about a One World Day poster? And a symbol, like the Olympic symbol? How about a mascot and a range of goods for sale: T-shirts, pens, bags, hats?

Drama and dance might also play a part. Could you write a short play which would express the ideas and values behind One World Day? Or invent a new dance for all to take part in?

Problems to consider

Are there any barriers to a celebration of One World Day? What factors divide our world? You might like to consider some of the following things which commonly cause problems:

language; culture; class; sex (male v female); age; mental and physical ability; poverty; nationality; religion

Finally, do not overlook climate: it may be monsoon in one place and mid-winter in another!

 Living Questions Teacher's Resource Book © 1993 Sue Hasted, Geoff Teece

RELATIONSHIPS

TEACHING NOTES

The pupils' book theme

Diversity is an obvious feature of human life. In contemporary societies, opportunities for living in close proximity with people who are significantly different from ourselves are expanding. These differences between people may either divide people from each other or be used to foster acceptable forms of community in which diversity is welcomed and, perhaps, celebrated.

Most of the major world religions have beliefs about what constitutes genuine community life. They also seek to promote the means by which this may be achieved. The examples selected for exploration of this theme are designed to help pupils develop their understanding of some of these beliefs. It is also intended in this theme to help pupils reflect on their own beliefs about how people with significant differences can or should live together.

In the first topic emphasis is placed on heightening the pupils' awareness of the complexity of the processes by which we acquire our distinctive individuality. It is also designed to help them reflect on the 'naturalness' of diversity as an outcome of such a process.

The second topic picks up the theme of individual and cultural differences, with the emphasis placed on the 'naturalness' of both unity and diversity in human life. Our shared or common human experience both unites and divides. The example of the orchestra introduces the concept of a 'community of communities'. This can simply be a description of the fact that within most communities there is a number of small sub-communities which cater for a range of different needs, interests, values and activities which members of the larger community may have. Different religious communities existing side by side in larger, pluralist societies are of this kind. The idea of a 'community of communities' can also suggest a quality of relationships between each of the sub-communities. Such relationships may reflect some common aspirations and identities which promote a mutual acceptance and appreciation of each other as members of the one nation or world. Multicultural societies strive for this quality of community life.

The second topic ends by challenging pupils to reflect on the possibility of such a harmonious society and on some of the possible obstacles to this. Such issues provoke some of the most important questions which our pupils will have to address as they grow older. One aspect of this is

explored further in the third topic, namely the particular problem of conflict in relationships. Pupils are encouraged to explore the beliefs and attitudes that lie at the roots of conflict.

The fourth topic focuses on a variety of ways in which relationships between people break down. It also provides an opportunity to explore a number of beliefs and practices which seek to repair such broken relationships. These include a number of examples from religions, most of which have central beliefs, teachings and practical programmes which offer guidance and help in all areas of life where broken human relations cause strife, ill-will and suffering.

The Activity sheets

1   The self-portraiture here could be set before reading the introduction to the section, done side-by-side with reading it, or afterwards. The point is not the glamour of the portrait but an awareness of the many relationships that construct us as individuals.

2   This worksheet is for initial group or class discussion, with questions 2 and 3 to be done privately by students, who may not wish to share their deepest beliefs in public. Its aim is to explore the ways in which such beliefs and values can conflict in particular circumstances, and to show that this may not mean that one belief is 'wrong' and another 'right'.

3   This is short debate about a subject that has occupied decades of discussion! The time limit ensures a productive outcome. Care should be taken to emphasise the positive side of all the religious statements involved, particularly in classes where a majority opinion could dominate; hence the need to divide the class without regard to actual opinion. Broadening the discussion out from family relationships, the aims here are to raise awareness of the way beliefs and values underlie everyday lives, and to link the family with the larger community in which this is also the case.

4   One way of investigating the nature of relationships is to look at contracts, which often spell out the underlying assumptions involved. Here we examine such assumptions by using the Jewish *ketuba* as the basis for a look at expectations in close relationships. This is extended to demonstrate the way in which relationship rights often imply responsibilities, a notion which applies at all levels of relationship.

5 This worksheet is background research for the section spread on relationships between communities, and could be done as homework, or as a group activity, after reading that spread. It is deliberately open-ended and could be used as a basis for a wall collage or display of findings, or simply as an individual study task. Students should be given appropriate warnings about interviewing strangers and should always go in pairs or small groups, or be accompanied by a responsible adult.

6 This brainstorming exercise allows students to uncover the beliefs that underlie individual conflicts. The teacher can bring out the fundamental nature of some of these beliefs, which may be answers to some of the ultimate questions human beings must all ask. It is also helpful to know that some of these beliefs conflict to such a degree that there is no compromise solution (for an older group, abortion is a good example here), while for others, compromises can be found (the issue of nuclear weapons might be a case in point).

7 Although this activity sheet touches on the subject of race, it is not about race but about conflicts between groupings within society (of which, of course, racial conflict can be one). The first aim is to explore the positive side of

difference, which is often missed, perhaps because negativity is more newsworthy. The second is for students to find out what each of the major religions has to say about conflict.

8 Again, a debate that has occupied the world since time began, but limited here to short, timed discussions of violence as a response in three arenas: the family, a particular society, and the international scene, with a vote after each one. It is interesting to bring out the factors which affect the vote in the three cases; one person may believe it is all right to smack a child, but not to fight a war, for example. Why?

9 There are many ways of solving conflict, but non-violent action is a particularly interesting one. Other modern examples include that of Gandhi, and, closer to home, the women of Greenham Common who protested against nuclear weapons. As an adjunct to this, it would be interesting to look at the Jain ideal of non-violence to all living beings, which leads them to sweep the streets free of invisible creatures before walking and to wear masks to avoid breathing them in. How far does one take non-violence? Does it extend to allowing disease organisms (malaria parasites, for example) the right to life? Students interested in animal rights may enjoy arguing this one through!

Self-portrait

Q **1** Take a piece of plain A4 paper and draw a self-portrait. It doesn't have to be artistic! Show the colours and shapes and textures of your face and hair. Add your favourite clothes and shoes. Leave some space around it to write things on later.

2 Round the edges of your self-portrait, try writing labels for the groups and comunities you belong to. You may find the following headings helpful: family, nation, race, religion, beliefs. You may find it difficult to label yourself; most people do. You can use question marks or leave it out. Often, the bits you are not sure about are the most interesting.

3 Add your interests and activities to your self-portrait. You could draw any equipment, too.

4 Do you have any aims to add to your self-portrait?

5 Is there anything else about you that makes you what you are? If you can think of anything, add that too.

6 Now you have completed a portrait of yourself as an individual - but only at this point in time. Have any of your characteristics changed over time? If so, make a note of them underneath the picture.

7 How many of the labels on your self-portrait involve relationships with other people? Try adding a tick after each one that does. Where did the ones that are left come from? Were you born with them?

Family values

Families have beliefs and values that hold them together. But sometimes these central beliefs can conflict with other beliefs.

Look at the extract below.

Moira wants to teach her children not to obey, but to stand up for themselves: "It makes a difference to be polite, but there's no need to be a doormat," she says.

Joy agrees. "I'd like to bring my children up with the values you need to be a good citizen. That means not littering the streets, and waiting your turn in the queue. But at the same time, I tell my eight-year-old girl that if she is too soft, people will take advantage - I'd like to know that she can survive when she is on her own."

As Chandra Malde of the Asian Family Counselling Service points out, these can be difficult distinctions for a child to make. "We Asians tell our children to behave in two ways: be polite at home and assertive at school. My sons used to tell me it was so confusing."

These parents are responding to a dangerous and competitive society where they daren't bring their children up to obey. Children need to be tough enough to look after themselves from an early age.

From 'Parents on the front line', an article by Madeleine Bunting in the *Guardian*, 17 September 1991

 Q *1 What do you think about this? Is it more important to be polite at all times and do what you are told, or to be assertive: to stand up for yourself? Discuss this in a small group.*

2 On your own, think about the way you were brought up and see if you can list at least three main beliefs or values that your family thought were important. They might be things like 'Do for others what you would like them to do for you', or 'Respect those who are older and know more about life than you do'. Or they might be more religious, such as 'Loving God and doing his will is more important than anything else', or 'There is something of God in everyone'.

3 If you had children of your own, what beliefs and values would be most important for you to pass on to them? Try to list three things you would teach your children. Would they be the same things you were taught, or different? Why?

Living Questions Teacher's Resource Book © 1993 Sue Hasted, Geoff Teece

Soap opera

Invent your own soap opera family!

Q 1   *Think up a name and a basic character for each of six people: Grandad, Grandma, Mother, Father, Daughter and Son. You can draw a sketch of them if it helps. Are they old or young? Bossy or timid? Miserly or generous? What do they like doing, or dislike doing?*

2   *Write a sentence for each of your characters which sums up their view of family life. Do they all agree? (At the bottom of the page are some beliefs about the nature of family life to help you think about this.)*

3   *Imagine the kind of house your family live in - is it a small semi, or a large country house? Are they in a village or a town? What jobs do the parents have, if any? What kind of school do the children attend?*

4   *A disaster happens to your little family. One of the members - you can decide who - is arrested for stealing. How does each member of the family react to this? What would each say? How would the family as a whole respond?*

When you have finished, read some of the stories aloud to the class. Discuss any differences the families' beliefs and values make to the ways in which they react to the problem.

As Christians, we are taught that we are part of God our Father's family. We are asked to love everyone, whatever life may bring; and that love is supposed to be forgiving, not selfish or proud. We always ask Jesus for help when things are difficult.

Our family is very close. As Jews we are expected to remember God and praise him at all times, and our family life reflects that, especially when we have our *Shabbat* meal together every week.

Because we're Muslims, our home is a very holy place, like the mosque. Praying together every day makes us very close, but we are also part of the larger Muslim community. Our family is quite strict, but that means we have a lot of respect for each other, too. I know I would be looked after, whatever I did.

We're not particularly religious in my family, but Mum and Dad brought us up to love each other and to respect everyone's right to be heard. I think everyone has something to contribute. You have to be tolerant of people's faults, but not to the extent of allowing them to be lazy or selfish.

We have an ideal of peace and unselfishness. Buddhists like us try to follow the middle way, not to indulge in anything, whether it be pleasures such as TV or food, or painful feelings such as anger. We try to be mindful of everything we do.

In our family, we don't make distinctions between brothers and sisters and cousins. My uncles and aunts are like extra parents to us, too. As Hindus we believe that good deeds will help release us from the cycle of births and deaths, so we try to act unselfishly towards each other.

Friendship contract

Many Jewish couples sign a *ketuba* or marriage contract when they marry. This document sets out what they can expect from each other, and also says what should happen if the relationship breaks down. An example is shown on the right.

> **Q** *Do you think it's a good idea to have a contract for a close relationship? What are the advantages and disadvantages?*

1   Imagine that you want to write a friendship contract for yourself and a good friend. With a partner, discuss what you might include in the contract and make a list of items to include. You might want to include things such as:

- *Always back me up in any argument*
- *Let me borrow your bike/watch (or other precious item)*
- *Always tell me when you think I'm being stupid.*

The groom and bride have also promised each other to strive throughout their lives together to achieve an openness which will enable them to share their thoughts and feelings and their experiences

To be sensitive at all times to each other's needs to attain mutual intellectual emotional physical and spiritual fulfillment, to work for the perpetuation of Judaism and of the Jewish people in their home, in their family life and in their communal endeavours

This marriage has been authorised also by the civil authorities of..................

It is valid and binding

witness............   witness............
bride..............   groom..............
              rabbi..................

2   Get together with another pair and put your two lists together. Do you agree with all the items on your joint list? If not, discuss them until you have a list you agree on.

3   Now ask yourselves why you have chosen each item. For instance, 'Always back me up in any argument' could be there because you think that loyalty to a friend is more important than whether that friend is right or wrong to be arguing. This is the belief or value you have.

4   Can you divide your list into 'rights' and 'responsibilities'? Often, the two go together in pairs. For instance, try the following:

a) My right to be liked by you is matched by my responsibility to....
b) My right to share your possessions is matched by my responsibility to .....
c) My right to your support at all times is matched by my responsibility to ....

5   What would make your relationship with a friend break down? Think of three things that would make you break a friendship contract.

   Living Questions Teacher's Resource Book © 1993 Sue Hasted, Geoff Teece

A community of communities

See if you can find out about the community of communities in which *you* live. You will have to do some research to find the answers. You may need a whole sheet of paper for each section!

Q **1 Family**
Note down any groups or organisations you and the other members of your close family belong to. These could be religious or secular (non-religious).

_____

_____

2 School
Note down any groups within your school. Then note down any larger groups your school may belong to.

_____

_____

3 City area, town or village
Note down any groups, societies or communities in your city area, town or village that you know about. Libraries, town halls and community centres, as well as health centres are good sources of information.

_____

_____

4 Nation
Note down the names of six national organisations you have heard of (there are far too many to collect them all).

_____

_____

5 Planet
Note down the names of six international or global organisations you have heard of (again, there are too many to collect them all).

_____

_____

6 *Now go through your collection and underline any that are religious.*
  • *What beliefs are they based on?*
  • *Are there any organisations that might conflict with each other? Why?*
  • *Do any of your organisations aim to resolve conflicts? Which ones? How do they go about it?*

Personal conflict brainstorm

Q **1** In a small group, brainstorm for five minutes as many reasons you can think of why individuals (not groups, communities or nations) conflict with each other. Note them down in the space below.

_____

_____

_____

_____

_____

_____

_____

2 Look at all the examples of conflicts. Underline any that are based on different beliefs about the way things are.

3 In your group, choose one of the conflicts you have underlined. Discuss the different beliefs that underlie that conflict until you can express them clearly in words. Then write down what those beliefs are.

_____

_____

_____

_____

_____

4 Now brainstorm solutions to the conflict for five minutes. Is there a compromise that can be reached, or are the beliefs so fundamentally different that no agreement can be reached? Can the conflicting individuals agree to disagree, or are there practical reasons why a solution must be found? Note down your conclusions below.

_____

_____

_____

_____

_____

_____

_____

 Living Questions Teacher's Resource Book © 1993 Sue Hasted, Geoff Teece

Racial conflict

Muslims believe that the diversity of race and colour to be found in the world is created by God. He has created this diversity for a reason: to help us learn to appreciate the separate identities of different groups and to respect them. By doing this we can learn about ourselves, too, and this makes us richer people.

Conflict based on racial prejudice is condemned in the Qur'an, which says that the world belongs to God and not to any particular race or nation. (You might like to read again the story of Bilal, to be found in the book *Muslims 2*.)

Q *1   Now leave racial groupings and international conflicts completely aside for the time being, and consider the following conflicts between groups in society. (Try to leave aside your own prejudices for the moment, too!) Pick one of the following groups of people who are often in conflict with each other:*

- *Vegetarians versus those who eat meat*
- *Noisy party enthusiasts versus those who want a quiet life*
- *Union members versus management*
- *School children and teachers*

What could each group have to learn from the other? What values does each group emphasise? Write the name of the two groups you have chosen on the left. Now write what they could teach each other on the right. If you have time, write about more than one pair.

Violence

When relationships break down, tempers rise. But is it ever justifiable to resort to violence? Opinions differ.

Most followers of the major religions believe that violence is justified in some circumstances, although not all agree. Some Christians, for example, believe that war can be justified, especially to prevent some greater evil; others, such as Quakers, are 'pacifists' who believe violence is never justified. Muslims believe that a war should only be started in self defence. Some Hindus and Sikhs believe that fighting for the truth is more important than non-violence. Guru Nanak, the first Sikh guru, said 'To fight and accept death for a righteous cause is the privilege of the brave and the truly religious.' Some religions such as Buddhism, however, place the emphasis more firmly on non-violence as a way of life.

1 *Discuss the following items in small groups. After five minutes' discussion for each one, take a class vote on whether the violence was justified.*

a) *Young John, age five, has been told a hundred times not to climb up on the bookshelves in the sitting room. One day, when his mother is in the kitchen, he does it again: and this time, the shelves all come down, ruining the wall and bruising John. His mother smacks him. Should she have done?*

b) *A particularly nasty murder has been committed: a young man has beaten an old lady to death while snatching her handbag, containing her pension money. In the country where this happens, the death penalty for murder is still in force. The young man is caught, tried, and found guilty. He is condemned to death. Should he die?*

c) *One nation, believing itself in the right over a land dispute, invades another. Other countries, believing it to be their duty to defend the invaded country from aggression, come to its aid. Armies and navies gather. War is declared. Many soldiers and civilians on both sides are killed. Eventually, the invaders are defeated, but at great cost to human life. Was the victory worth it?*

You might wish to look up the following references to explore further the ideas of the major religions on this subject.

- Judaism and Christianity: Torah (or Old Testament in the Bible), Deuteronomy 7: 1-16, 20: 10-18
- Islam: Qur'an, Sura 2: 216
- Christianity: The Bible, Matthew 5: 43-45 and 26: 47-52
- Hinduism: Bhagavad Gita 2: 31-32

 Living Questions Teacher's Resource Book © 1993 Sue Hasted, Geoff Teece

Martin Luther King

In the late 1950s, Martin Luther King was a Christian Baptist minister in Alabama, USA. In those days, especially in the southern United States, there were many laws which separated black and white people. Black people had originally been brought as slaves to the country by whites. The 'segregation' laws prevented them from voting, and they were not allowed to sit in the same areas as whites in buses and restaurants. Schools too were segregated. Often black people who annoyed whites were beaten up, or killed. Groups such as the Ku Klux Klan preached 'white power' and the superiority of the white 'race'. The police and the courts were dominated by whites, many of whom joined in the violence against blacks.

As a Christian, Martin Luther King decided that he should use non-violent action to protest against the unfair laws. This meant peaceful demonstrations, and peaceful disobedience of the laws. Anyone who joined his movement was risking injury and death. In his work for 'civil rights', King made many enemies, and was sent to jail several times, but he refused to use violent methods to achieve his aims.

From 1955 to 1956, Martin Luther King led a boycott of all the buses in Montgomery, Alabama. People refused to use the buses in protest against the segregation of black and white passengers. Eventually, segregation was declared illegal.

In 1963, King led 250,000 people on a march in Washington DC. He made a speech that has become famous, in which he said "I have a dream that one day this nation will rise up and live out the true meaning of its creed: *We hold these truths to be self-evident: that all men are created equal*". He won the Nobel Peace Prize in 1964, the year that racial discrimination was finally outlawed throughout the USA.

Martin Luther King was assassinated in 1968.

1 Do you know of any other examples of non-violent protest? Did they achieve their aims? Might these aims have been achieved by other methods?

2 Some people call themselves 'pacifists', meaning that they will never use violence in any circumstances. If they are Christians, like Dr King, or Jews, they may point to the sixth commandment 'You shall not commit murder' (Exodus 20:2-17) Such people are often asked what they would do if a member of their close family were attacked in their presence. What would you do?

STAGES OF LIFE

TEACHING NOTES

The pupils' book theme

The shared human experience of passing through a series of different stages of life, each with its own broad characteristics and needs, has prompted people in all generations and cultures to develop symbolic ideas and images of life. In general terms, each of these images reflects some deeply held beliefs and values about human life.

The topics chosen for the development of this theme are designed to engage pupils in a consideration of different images of life and the beliefs and values which they encapsulate. They also provide opportunities to explore ideas about behaviour patterns and activities considered to be appropriate at different stages of life and to examine some of the ways in which seemingly fortuitous events shape our lives.

In this section pupils are given opportunities to explore several ways in which various people and religious traditions express some of their thoughts, feelings, attitudes and beliefs about the stages of life through which people pass.

The first topic provides an opportunity for an exploration of a number of images of life which provide for many people a way of expressing a comprehensive understanding of how all the diverse and complex features of life may be held together in a cohesive pattern or purpose. Some of these images of life can also be sources of inspiration, challenge, security and hope for people living a complex and rapidly changing modern life.

The following images are explored to emphasise the significance of the physical and temporal life-span of individuals: 'Life is like a journey'; 'Life is like a river'; 'Life is like an hourglass'. Other images highlight the continuity of life from generation to generation and express particular beliefs about this process, for example, images of seeds and plants; caterpillar, chrysalis, butterfly; circles without beginning or end. In the second topic these images are linked to religious beliefs as expressed by adherents of a variety of faiths at different stages of life.

In the third topic, links are made between the fortuitous aspects of life and, for example, beliefs in the will of God or Allah, the guidance of the Holy Spirit, the laws of *karma*, fate, luck, etc. This topic is designed to help pupils explore how the choices we make now, whether individual or collective, personal or public, can affect the future. This highlights the relationship between many of our choices for immediate action or inaction, and the

future shape and quality of life for ourselves and following generations.

The fourth topic takes up the ideas developed in the third, and relates them to moral and ethical standards and how they function in regard to behaviour patterns considered appropriate at different stages of life. Suggestions for follow-up work encourage pupils to explore how these ideas relate to beliefs in people's lives. Pupils will see how these ideas are linked to the ways in which people appeal to beliefs in the will or call of God when making decisions about an appropriate time to engage in some major activity, profession or vocation.

The Activity sheets

1 The aim of this worksheet is to prompt reflection on the images of life discussed in the pupils' book and to help pupils express their own intuition about the progress of human life.

2 If audio tapes of *The Hitchiker's Guide To the Galaxy* are available, this extract could be played to the class. It provides two more images of life to consider along with the others in the pupils' book, and shows how people try to make sense of the evidence available to them in order to decide on their response to the fact of being alive. It also usefully provides a way in to the main differences between the Judaeo/Christian/Islamic linear view of life, and the Hindu/Buddhist circular view.

3 Using information from the Westhill Project books *Christians 3*, *Muslims 3* and *Jews 3* and the photopacks on the six faith traditions, pupils can use this chart to note similarities and differences in approach to the main stages of human life. It is important to bring out the main beliefs that are demonstrated in the various ceremonies chosen.

4 It is worth collecting some recent newspaper headlines or aid agency material on natural and man-made disasters (Oxfam, Christian Aid, Greenpeace etc.) for a background display before using this worksheet, especially where these show responses such as 'it is the will of Allah' or 'we could have chosen to avoid this'. The story represents a point of view that most who have Western cultural values will find very alien, and this provides a useful defamiliarising stimulus for discussion. The aim is to raise the question about the dividing line between 'fate' or 'the will of God' and human responsibility. At what point does choice enter in?

5 This sheet provides a bit of fun to start the ball rolling when considering the idea of choices for action leading to consequences which provide further choices, and so forth. Although some members of the group may be tempted to make the sequences absurd, it should be possible to allow a serious discussion of cumulative consequences after the laughter. The Jewish mystical idea of *tikkun olam* (see book), as well as the ideas of eventual reward and punishment, or of *karma* for future lives, can be brought out here.

6 The research work suggested here has to be approached with sensitivity, as the questions are very personal. An alternative way of managing it would be to invite three or four representatives of different religious traditions in to class to answer the questions all together, having prepared them beforehand. The imaginative essay suggested is meant to develop reflection on, and understanding of, the kinds of choices made at various stages in life.

7 This is a 'balloon debate' of sorts which focusses on the values behind the choices we make, and also relates them to stages of life. It is worth working through this quickly, limiting time for discussions, to avoid argument about such abstractions as 'love' leading to confusion. Before starting, give a few concrete examples of each value to help crystallize opinions. Allow additions to the list if they arise. Working in small groups, perhaps with a plenary session, will make it easier for some children to express their ideas.

8 The story of Guru Nanak's calling is given to illustrate the idea of vocation or purpose in life. Other examples of ways in which people of different faiths express a sense of purpose in life can be found in the Westhill Project pupils' books, e.g. *Christians 3* p.54, *Jews 3* p.13. Collecting examples of famous people with a strong sense of purpose (based on beliefs which may or may not be religious) affords the opportunity for understanding a range of expressions of this sense.

9 Designing your own rite of passage is one way of summing up the work done on stages of life in this chapter. By way of background to this worksheet, it may be helpful to discuss the ages at which people are legally allowed to do such things as leave school, claim social security benefits, work, drive, marry without consent, vote, etc. In Western society, no one age is accepted as the point of transition to adulthood, and such secular rites as there are tend to be fragmented. Religious initiation rites seem to take place (in general) at an earlier age than most Western secular passages into adulthood. Why should this be so? What does it actually mean to be grown up? What recognition of adulthood would be desirable? What are the consequences of lack of recognition by older people? Pupils will need to have thought about the purpose of life and their own values in order to decide what items they would wish to select for their celebration, which could be religious, secular, or a mixture.

Images of life

Q **1** *What do think think the composer of this nursery rhyme thought about human life? Why do you think she or he compared it to the days of one short week?*

If you were to think up an image to describe Solomon's life, you might compare it to a firework rocket, rushing upwards as it burns, exploding into a shower of sparks and then falling slowly back to earth, its flame burned out.

Solomon Grundy
Born on Monday
Christened on Tuesday
Married on Wednesday
Took ill on Thursday
Worse on Friday
Died on Saturday
Buried on Sunday
This is the end of
Solomon Grundy.

2 In the space below, draw your idea of the main shape of human life. Keep to a simple shape. You might like to use one of the images discussed in the pupils' book, p.33, or to think up your own diagram.

Which stages of life, or events in life, do you consider important? Note them down in the space around your diagram.

3 Using your notes and your image of human life, see if you can write a short poem expressing your ideas. It doesn't have to rhyme.

What is life?

Two missiles following a spaceship have suddenly changed into a whale and a bowl of petunias and are falling to earth...

...this poor innocent creature had very little time to come to terms with its identity as a whale before it then had to come to terms with not being a whale any more. This is a complete record of its thought from the moment it began its life until the moment it ended it.

'Ah ...! What's happening?' it thought. 'Er, excuse me, who am I? Hello? Why am I here? What's my purpose in life? What do I mean by who am I? Calm down now, get a grip now ... oh! this is an interesting sensation, what is it? It's a sort of ... yawning, tingling sensation in my ... my ... well I suppose I'd better start finding names for things if I want to make any headway in what, for the sake of what I shall call an argument, I shall call the world, so let's call it my stomach.

Good. Ooooh, it's getting quite strong. And hey, what about this whistling roaring sound going past what I'm suddenly going to call my head? Perhaps I can call that ... wind! Is that a good name? It'll do ... perhaps I can find a better name for it later when I've found out what it's for....

Hey! What's this thing? This ... let's call it a tail - yeah, tail. Hey! I can really thrash it around pretty good, can't I? Wow! Wow! That feels great! Doesn't seem to achieve very much but I'll probably find out what it's for later on. Now, have I built up any coherent picture of things yet?

No. Never mind, hey, this is really exciting, so much to find out about, so much to look forward to, I'm quite dizzy with anticipation... Or is it the wind? There really is a lot of that now isn't there?

And wow! Hey! What's this thing suddenly coming towards me very fast? Very, very fast. So big and flat and round, it needs a big, wide-sounding name like ... ow ... ound ... round ... ground! That's it! That's a good name - ground! I wonder if it will be friends with me?'

And the rest, after a sudden wet thud, was silence.

Curiously enough, the only thing that went through the mind of the bowl of petunias as it fell was 'Oh no, not again.' Many people have speculated that, if we knew exactly why the bowl of petunias had thought that, we would know a lot more about the nature of the universe than we do now.

From *The Hitchhiker's Guide to the Galaxy* by Douglas Adams

Q 1 Read the extract above.

2 The whale has a very short time to find out what life is, and what its purpose in life is, before it meets its sudden end. Could the whale be rather like a person, born into the world and trying to make sense of it? Imagine it meets a Jew, a Christian and a Muslim. What would each one tell it about the purpose of life?

3 The bowl of petunias thinks it has been through this experience before. Which religious faiths hold that people live many lives? What would their representatives tell the petunias about the meaning of life?

Progress though life

Q **1** *Choose two major religions. Write them in the boxes below. Then research how each of them approaches the major events in a person's life. Do they have special festivals or ceremonies for them? Write notes in the spaces provided.*

Birth		
Initiation (becoming adult)		
Marriage		
Death		

2   What does each believe is the purpose of life?
What main patterns of belief about the purpose of life can you find in the research you have done about each of the religions you have chosen?

                    Living Questions Teacher's Resource Book © 1993 Sue Hasted, Geoff Teece

Life's chances and how we view them

THE WISE FATHER

A poor farmer's horse ran off into the country of the barbarians. All his neighbours offered their condolences, but his father said 'How do you know that this isn't good fortune?' After a few months the horse returned with a barbarian horse of excellent stock. All his neighbours offered their congratulations, but his father said 'How do you know that this isn't a disaster?' The two horses bred, and the family became rich in fine horses. The farmer's son spent much of his time riding them; one day he fell off and broke his hipbone. All his neighbours offered the farmer their condolences, but his father said, 'How do you know that this isn't good fortune?' Another year passed, and the barbarians invaded the frontier. All the able-bodied young men were conscripted, and nine-tenths of them died in the war. Thus good fortune can be disaster and vice versa. Who can tell how events will be transformed?

From the *Huai Nan Tzu*

Q 1 Read the story above on your own.

2 In a small group, discuss whether you agree with the conclusion in the story that there are no 'good' or 'bad' events.

3 Jews, Christians and Muslims often speak of events as being the result of 'the will of God'. Hindus and some Buddhists may speak of events as being fated, or the result of karma (past actions). Talk about these ideas. Do you think they might influence the way in which people react to events?

4 In your group, choose a recent 'chance' such as:

- a volcanic explosion which took, or threatened to take, lives
- a catastrophic storm or flood
- an earthquake
- a pollution accident such as an oil spill.

Talk about your responses to the event. Was it an 'act of God' or a 'natural phenomenon'? Why do you think so? Could it have been avoided if people had made different choices about their actions?

Open consequences

Most of us believe in free will: we believe that we can choose how to respond to what life has presented us with and so, to some extent, we can plan and develop our lives as we go along.

The alternative is to think of oneself as a powerless victim of circumstances beyond one's control, and be resigned to fate. Occasionally, we do think something like this; then we are tempted to say 'but it's not my fault' or 'it isn't fair' instead of taking responsibility for our lives.

Even the smallest choice of action can be very important. Say you decide to go to the cinema instead of doing your homework. At the cinema you see such a great film that you decide you will become a film-maker when you are older. Grown up and now a film-maker, you decide to specialise in films about wildlife and conservation. Researching a film on lions, you meet your future partner, a zoologist...and so on.

Islam, Christianity and Judaism very clearly stand by human responsibility for choosing the right actions in life. All major religions have developed rules to help people make the right choices. Those religions such as Hinduism and Buddhism which describe human life in terms of 'fate' or *karma* also emphasize that humans can choose their responses to circumstances.

Try playing 'open consequences'. At the top of a piece of paper write a name and a brief description of a character.

Pass the paper to the person next to you. Their job is to write the next short sentence, which must describe a choice the character made about something she or he did. Try to make it fit the character described. They then pass it on to the next person.

Person 3 adds another sentence describing a choice which follows on from the one in the previous sentence, and passes it on to person 4, who adds another choice, and so on. The only rule is that each choice must follow on from the last one. Stop at person 6. Person 6 reads everything that has been written and adds the consequence of all the choices.

You could take the game in a negative or a positive direction. An alternative is to play the game with a partner. One takes the role of 'goodie' and always makes a good choice of action; the other plays 'baddie' and always makes a bad choice. Take turns to start!

- Danny Jones, schoolboy age 12
- Decided to sell his bike and buy a computer games system
- He played for hours every day
- He missed his tea most days
- He never spoke to the rest of his family
- He became so unfit he was dropped from the football team and his mum banned the computer games.

        Living Questions Teacher's Resource Book © 1993 Sue Hasted, Geoff Teece

Personal choices research

You are going to interview someone a good bit older than yourself. Choose someone you know well, who will not mind answering some personal questions and taking part in your survey. Their name should not be put down on the paper. If they don't want to answer a particular question, leave it and go on to the next. Try to ask further questions in response to their answers, so that you get an impression of the reasons why they made their choice.

School choices

Do you think you chose your friends well when you were at school? Why, or why not?

Which subjects did you choose to work at, and which did you choose to give up? Why?

What other activities did you choose to take part in at school?

Work choices

Why did you choose to go into your particular kind of work?

Would you ever choose to change your job?

What do you like about your work? What do you dislike?

Partnership choices

Why did you choose your partner? (Or, if single: Did you choose not to have a partner? If so, why?)

Was having children (or not having children) a deliberate choice?

What do you like about being together (or being single)?

General

What was the best choice you ever made? What was the worst?

Would you make any different choices if you could start again?

Q 1 The choices we make in life often reflect our beliefs about the purpose of life. Can you see any particular pattern of beliefs in the answers your interviewee has given you?

2 Imagine you are looking back at your own life from the vantage point of old age. Using the questions above to help you, write about the decisions you made during your schooldays; your partner (if any); and your job, and why you chose them.

Morals and standards at different times in our lives

Q 1 Below, you will find a list of statements about beliefs or values that many people of all faiths consider important. Read them through carefully. Then place them in order of significance: number 1 for the one you consider most important, 2 for the next, and so on.

If you are working as a group, a good way to do this is to start backwards. Which value is the least important? Debate for a few minutes, then vote to 'throw away' one value, then another and another, until you are left with the five most important.

- Love for others
- Respect for others' views
- Respect for others' property
- Respect for others' bodies
- Respect for animals
- Justice
- Kindness
- Charity or help for others
- Faithfulness or loyalty in a relationship
- Truthfulness
- Moderation (i.e. not indulging in anything to excess)

2 Look at your top five values. Is there a particular emphasis on any of these when you are young, middle-aged, or old? Write them down in the order of importance you think is appropriate for each of three ages:

	Value	Youth	Middle age	Old age
1				
2				
3				
4				
5				

3 If your order of importance changes with age, why do you think some things are more important than others at different stages in life?

Living Questions Teacher's Resource Book © 1993 Sue Hasted, Geoff Teece

Vocation

People sometimes feel themselves called to live life in a certain way, as a result of a spiritual experience. One example was Guru Nanak, the first Sikh guru.

THE CALLING OF GURU NANAK

Nanak was born in 1469 near Lahore, in the Punjab, northern India. He grew up as a Hindu, but at the time, his country was ruled by Muslims, and eventually he went to work as an accountant for a government official who followed Islam.

One day Nanak went to take a morning swim in the local river, as most Hindus did. When he did not return, it was feared that he had drowned. The river was dragged, but his body was not found. After three days, when everyone had given up hope, Nanak turned up - with an amazing story.

He had been to the court of God himself, he said. There he had been given a cup of sweet nectar to drink, and he was told to rejoice in God's name and teach others to do the same. From that day onwards he was known as Guru - teacher, or spiritual guide. He gave up his job and for many years he travelled the country, teaching, until he settled down and formed the first Sikh community.

Guru Nanak's calling is an example of the way in which some people dedicate their lives to a particular course they feel has been chosen for them by God.

 1 Try to find out about someone who has felt called to live in a particular way. They could be a personal friend or someone famous, such as Mother Teresa of Calcutta or the Dalai Lama of Tibet.

Marking passages in life

In many cultures and religions, moving from one stage of life to another is celebrated in various ways. Most religions have ceremonies to mark 'rites of passage' at important times in life: for example, admission as a full member of the Jewish community happens at Bar or Bat Mitzvah. Birth, marriage and death also often have ceremonies, too.

Such 'rites of passage' have some things in common. The people who are changing from one state to the next may:

- be marked out as special in some way (often by dress)

- spend a period of time withdrawn or separate from the community before joining it (or leaving it)
- have to learn something new, often some new rules for living
- have to make some promises, or prove themselves worthy in some way
- have a celebration or party to welcome them into the new community, or as they leave the old community.

You can do the following either by yourself, or in a group.

 **1 Work out your own 'rite of passage' to mark your arrival at adulthood. First, decide when you think it should be celebrated. How old should you be?**

2 Decide how you would be marked out as special for the duration of the celebrations. Would you have a special dress or uniform of some kind? Design it.

3 How would you separate yourself from society before your celebration? Where would you go, and for how long? How would you use the time?

4 Decide what you would need to learn for your new role as an adult in society. Make two lists: first, the practical things you need to know to act as an adult in Britain today, and second, at least three basic rules of conduct that you would agree to live by. You can use the rules from any of the major world religions if you wish.

5 Either: Write a promise that you would make at the ceremony of welcome. This should express your beliefs about the purpose of life. Or: Devise a test that you would have to pass to prove that you were worthy to join adult society.

6 Design a ceremony of welcome for new adults. Who would be present, and what would they do? Would there be food and drink? Would there be music? How would the promise fit in? How would your changed status as a new adult be demonstrated publicly?

LIFESTYLES

TEACHING NOTES

The pupils' book theme

Lifestyles are seldom static. They change with our circumstances. They are shaped by changes in such things as age, family size and commitments, occupation, wealth, health and national/ geographical environment. They also reflect personal ambitions, hopes and fears and what are perceived to be the essential ingredients of 'the good life'.

The topics selected for the exploration of this theme focus on beliefs, religious and otherwise, about what constitutes the good life. They also provide opportunities for an examination of a range of behaviour patterns and events which either contribute to or inhibit the realisation of a good life for all people.

In the first topic, the pupils are encouraged to gather examples of images of the good life. These can come from a range of sources, such as TV and other commericals, literature, music, art and drama. The examples collected in the first topic can then be put alongside religious images of the good life in the second topic, drawn from Christianity and Buddhism, some of which look for some future or supernatural time and place when such a good life may be fully realised.

The third topic focuses more on the ways and means of improving the quality of life for people in the here and now. Clearly, these will reflect beliefs about the nature of the good life and the pupils may be helped to reflect on the logical and practical relationships between the ends and the means used to achieve such ends.

The fourth topic also brings together beliefs about the good life and some of the factors in our 'here and now' experience which threaten the quality of life for significant numbers of people. An important feature of this topic is the emphasis on helping pupils extend their reflection to beliefs about how present lifestyles may threaten the realisation of some future good life.

The Activity sheets

1 The aim of this activity sheet is to get students talking about what the basic necessities of human life are. Obviously we need food and shelter. But what else? Is medicine more important than music, the food of the soul?

2 The point is made in the section that much of our information about 'the good life' comes to us through the media. In fact, students do not consume the media uncritically and will be well aware of the difference between an advertisement which tries to sell them something and a soap opera which may include generally-accepted images of desirable possessions and ways of life. The aim here is not to 'innoculate' students against the power of the media. It is simply to use the media as a focus for their own ideas about what is desirable.

3 This worksheet mimics the star profiles found in teen magazines. It is another way of looking at what is desirable, but this time with the emphasis more on lifestyles, beliefs and values than on possessions. It should be noted that appearance is often, but not always, a useful indicator of values.

4 In the section we looked at a Buddhist lifestyle which deliberately repudiates possessions and attachments and sees the aim of life as awakening to awareness. Here the idea is to investigate the consequences of the Buddhist values for everyday life. Our society commonly breaks all the rules in the Five Precepts: why? What values are expressed in our lifestyles, and how do they contrast with the Buddhists'?

5 The description of one young woman's decision to become a nun allows students to look at Jesus's commandments about how humans should live. These can be related to those of other traditions who choose to live in poverty: Buddhist monks and nuns or those of other faiths who eschew possessions, and ordinary people who decide that other values are more important than accumulating wealth.

6 The Sikh story of Guru Nanak and the rich man is the starting point for an investigation of the attitudes of the world religions to wealth.

7 The idea of this activity sheet is to help students understand that beliefs and values underlie the kinds of improvements we want to make to the quality of life. Indeed, the idea that progress is possible and is a good thing is in itself a belief. A class comparison of individuals' ideas should also show that people may want to do the same thing for quite different reasons of belief or value.

8 The work of charities and pressure groups is always based on beliefs about the nature of life, human rights and the duties of people to be reponsible for each other. This activity sheet looks at two and relates their work back to religious beliefs about such things. It could be useful to invite a speaker from a local charity or

pressure group to explore this aspect of their work with the class. Some, e.g. Christian Aid, can provide excellent videos which bring out the relationship between beliefs and lifestyles.

9   The passage from the New Testament quoted here seems to be quite clear that there are specific actions to be undertaken by Christians to help others, and that their lives will be judged on how well they have carried them out. Although the sheet has a practical focus, asking students to think about what these instructions might actually mean in present circumstances, it also raises a question which the more able may find interesting: do we do what we think is right because it is right, or because we will get a reward if we do it and a punishment if we do not?

Desert island basics

Imagine you are marooned alone on a desert island. It is a typical cartoon desert island: there is no food or fresh water, and only one coconut palm for shade from the hot sun.

Q **1 Before you leave the sinking ship that brought you to the island, you can choose to bring with you five items from the following list. Pick the five that would allow you to live the kind of life you would most like to live in the circumstances.**

- Building materials: wood, hammer and nails
- Tins of food and drink and tin opener
- Matches
- Hat
- Crate of bottles of alcohol
- A human companion
- Lethal poison pill for a painless death
- Barrel of water
- Telescope

- Medicine for all basic needs plus DIY doctor's book
- Radio and transmitter
- One bale of strong cotton cloth
- Shoes
- Solar-power operated record player and eight records
- Book (you can choose the title)
- Sleeping bag
- A pet (cat, dog, parrot or whatever)
- Paper and pencils

2 Would you try to escape or wait to be rescued? How would you pass the time while you were marooned? What would you enjoy about your situation? What would you dislike?

What makes 'the good life'?

Q *1 Choose:*
- *one TV drama programme (e.g. an episode of Neighbours)*
- *one advertisement you like (from TV or anywhere else)*

Thinking about them carefully, try to fill in the following chart.

Name of TV programme

Name of a 'good' character in programme:

What do you like about their lifestyle?

Name of a 'bad' character in programme:

What do you dislike about their lifestyle?

Has the programme anything to tell you about how to live a good life? If so, how would you sum up its message?

Advertisement for   (product name)

What do you like about this advert?

Would you buy the product yourself? If so, what would it do for you?

What does the advert tell you about 'the good life'?

2   Select a magazine of your choice. Take a piece of paper and divide it vertically in two, with the headings 'good' and 'bad'.

Working through the magazine, list under 'good' any positive images of lifestyles shown in the magazine. These could be, for example, nice clothes, a happy person working with disabled kids, a desirable holiday in Disneyworld, an expensive car, etc.

List under 'bad' any negative images you may find, for example kids living in sewers in Colombia, drug addicts, ugly person before new make-up is put on, etc.

How does the 'good life' shown in the magazine compare with your own? What things does it make you want?

   Living Questions Teacher's Resource Book © 1993 Sue Hasted, Geoff Teece

Role models

Most people can think of someone they admire. It could be a music star or a film star, or someone on TV; it could be someone in your family or a close friend, or someone older you want to be like. Who do you admire?

 1 Pick a role model and fill in the questionnaire.

Name:

Description of looks:

Job:

Where they live:

Favourite things (e.g. colours, food, pets, music etc):

What he or she does best:

I like   (name) because

Things I do the same as   (name):

My other favourite people are:

 **2 Do any of your role models lead the sort of life you would like to lead? What do you like about their lifestyles? What do you disapprove of? Why?**

The Five Precepts

Q 1 Below are the Five Precepts which Buddhists promise to follow. Look at them carefully and make notes beside each one on the practical consequences of keeping them. What sorts of things would you not be able to do, and what would you have to do?

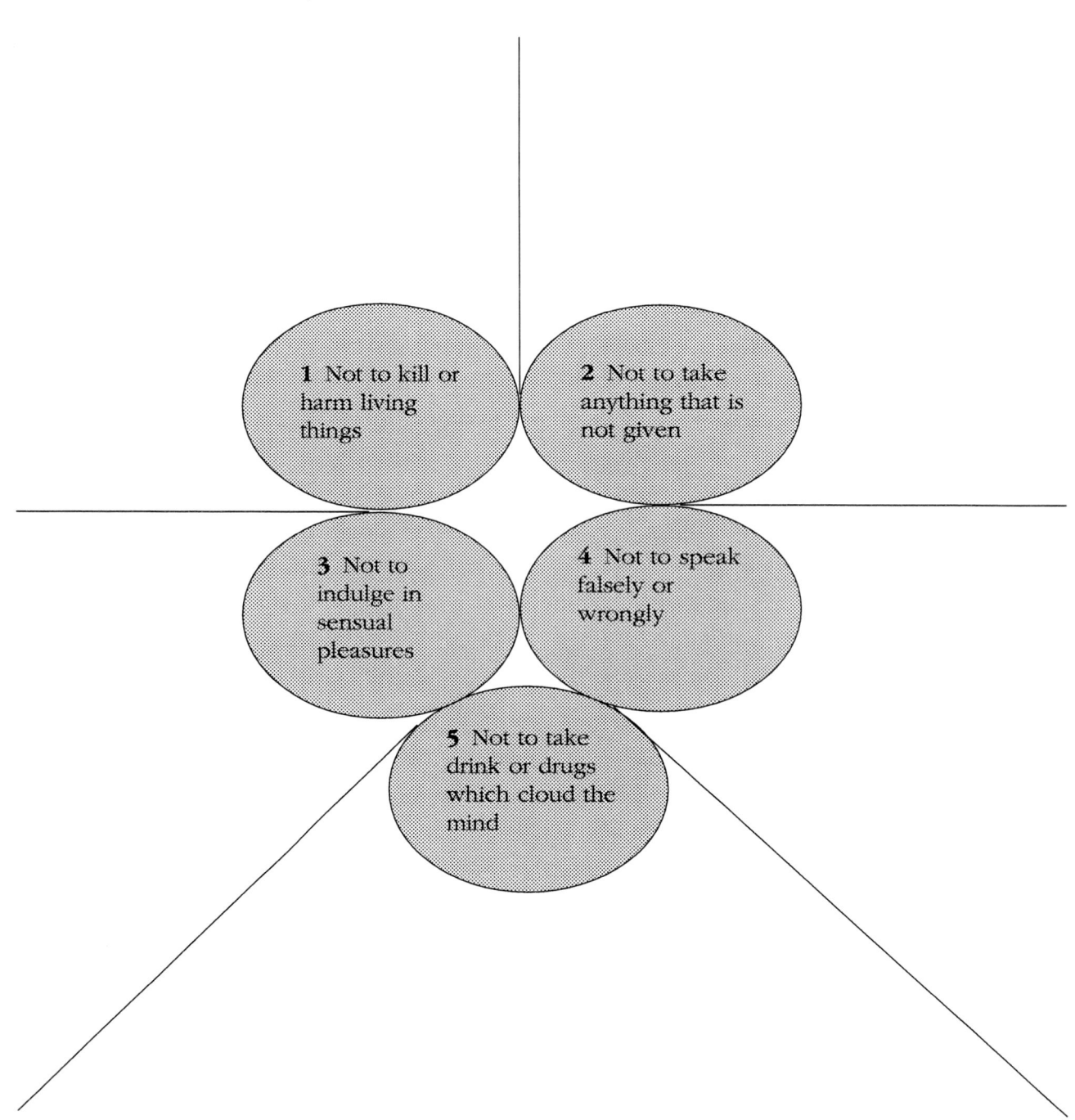

1 Not to kill or harm living things

2 Not to take anything that is not given

3 Not to indulge in sensual pleasures

4 Not to speak falsely or wrongly

5 Not to take drink or drugs which cloud the mind

2 Now pool your thoughts in a small group (or with the class as a whole). Talk about the differences that keeping these rules would make to modern life if everyone were Buddhist. What do you think a Buddhist's attitude to being rich would be?

 Living Questions Teacher's Resource Book © 1993 Sue Hasted, Geoff Teece

Choosing poverty

Some people live in poverty because life has dealt them a bad hand of cards: they could be unemployed, or homeless, for example. But there are some people who choose to be poor. Here's one young woman who has chosen to become a Roman Catholic nun. She will 'take vows' (make promises to God) of poverty, chastity and obedience, and dedicate herself to a life of service to others.

'For Joanne Blake, the strangest part of training to be a nun is her work selling yoghurt to commuters. Every morning after prayers at the Sisters of Mercy convent in London's East End, Joanne, age 19, rushes off to work at a cafe in Liverpool Street Station.

"The sisters want me to have an idea of the world I'm giving up," Joanne explains in a light Irish lilt. The 15 nuns at the convent also expect the young 'associate' to gain qualifications. Next year she'll start an English A Level, and she plans to train as a teacher before taking her vows.

Although she can still back out, Joanne is determined not to. "I've wanted to become a nun since I was a very little girl."

None of the commuters and workmates around her would think to label her as a trainee nun. Those who discover her religious feelings think she is mad and usually tell her so. "But I explain to them that this is my way of life. It's fulfilling, but in a different sort of way." Like? "You're available to everybody without belonging to anybody," she says. "You're free. You don't speak the gospel, you don't preach the gospel, you *are* the gospel."

Joanne's family at home in County Offaly are proud of her decision. But she finds the hushed respect on visits stifling. "When I come home they get out the best china. I have to tell them to give me a mug, for God's sake!"

From Julie Johnson's article 'Habit for Life', Young EGO, the *Guardian* 15 October 1991.

Q **1 In what ways is Joanne following the advice of Jesus about lifestyle? What is she prepared to give up? What does she think she will gain by becoming a nun?**

2   Can you think of any other examples of people who choose to be poor? Why do they do so?

Guru Nanak and the rich man

One day Nanak was invited to dinner by a very rich man called Dunni Chand. As they were relaxing after the meal, Dunni Chand asked "Is there anything I can do for you? I am very wealthy, and I would be happy to give you anything you would like."

Nanak smiled and then took a needle from his pocket. "Yes", he said. "I would be grateful if you would give me this needle when we meet in the next world, after our deaths."

Dunni Chand did not know what to say.

"But - how can I take the needle to the next world?" he stammered.

"If a little thing like a needle cannot be taken to the next world, what about all your riches?" Nanak asked. "Only your good deeds go with you when you die. Money is worthless unless it is used for the good of other people."

Dunni Chand realised then how wise Nanak was. After that, he gave away all his possessions and spent the rest of his life helping the poor.

Q 1 *Most of the world religions have something to say about riches and what to do with them. What other examples can you think of? Note them down below.*

_____

_____

_____

_____

_____

_____

_____

_____

2 If someone today decided to give up wealth in order to help others, what sorts of work could they do? List as many kinds of work as you can.

_____

_____

_____

_____

_____

_____

_____

_____

_____

Living Questions Teacher's Resource Book © 1993 Sue Hasted, Geoff Teece

Improving the quality of life

 1 In the left-hand column below, list three things that would improve the quality of personal life, local community life, and national or international life.

Then, opposite each one in the right-hand column, work out what belief each of your recommendations is based on. We have included one example in each section to show you the idea. Remember, there are no 'right' answers, and there can be different beliefs which result in the same action.

Things I would do to improve...	Because I believe...
Personal life	
Do a good deed every day	I would be a better person
1	
2	
3	
Local community life	
More facilities for young people	It would keep them out of trouble
1	
2	
3	
National/international life	
A new peace-keeping force	War is a bad thing
1	
2	
3	

Helping others

Many organisations exist to help people who are poor, homeless, starving, or the victims of disasters such as war, earthquake and famine. Here are two.

Oxfam

Oxfam is a development and relief agency. It provides emergency relief in times of crisis, but is also concerned with long-term sustainable development.

By funding local groups, regardless of race, sex, religion or politics, Oxfam supports people's struggle to survive and improve the quality of life for themselves and their families.

The organisation is independent of government and depends largely on voluntary work and donations from the public to continue its work with those people most acutely afflicted by poverty.

Shelter

Shelter is a national campaigning group for homeless people. It provides practical help for people with housing problems through an expanding national network of housing aid centres, where expert advice on homelessness, benefits, landlord and tenant disputes, disrepair, mortgage debt and other problems is offered.

Shelter also offers 'care and repair' schemes to enable elderly people to stay in their own homes by improving and decorating them.

Shelter campaigns to change government policies and attitudes to bad housing and homelessness. It conducts research and lobbies the government and MPs to expose the failures of the housing system and promote alternative policies and better practices.

Q

1　People of many religious groups contribute to the work of both Oxfam and Shelter. What beliefs would make them want to do this? Can you find any statements from the faith traditions that support those beliefs?

2　What other charities or pressure groups exist to improve the quality of life? Choose two more and write a short description of what they do. Do any of the religions support their work? Why?

The good life and the future

The following passage is from the Bible. It is one of the sayings of Jesus reported in the Gospel according to Matthew.

'When the Son of Man comes in his glory and all the angels with him, he will sit in state on his throne, and all the nations gathered before him. He will separate men into two groups as a shepherd separates the sheep from the goats, and he will place the sheep on his right hand and the goats on his left. Then the king will say to those on his right hand, "You have my father's blessing; come, enter and possess the kingdom that has been ready for you since the world was made. For when I was hungry you gave me food; when thirsty, you gave me drink; when I was a stranger you took me into your home, when naked you clothed me; when I was ill you came to my help, when in prison you visited me." Then the righteous will reply, "Lord, when was it that we saw you hungry and fed you, or thirsty and gave you drink, a stranger and took you home, or naked and clothed you? When did we see you ill or in prison, and come to visit you?" And the king will answer, "I tell you this: anything you did for one of my brothers here, however humble, you did for me."

'Then he will say to those on his left hand, "The curse is upon you; go from my sight to the eternal fire which is ready for the devil and his angels. For when I was hungry you gave me nothing to eat, when thirsty nothing to drink; when I was a stranger you gave me no home, when naked you did not clothe me; when I was ill and in prison you did not come to my help." And they too will reply, "Lord, when was it that we saw you hungry or thirsty or a stranger or naked or ill or in prison, and did nothing for you?" And he will answer, "I tell you this: anything you did not do for one of these, however humble, you did not do for me." And they will go away to eternal punishment, but the righteous will enter eternal life.'

Matthew 24: 31-46

 1 Make a list of examples of people, in our society or the rest of the world, who are:
- *hungry or thirsty*
- *strangers or homeless*
- *have no means to buy clothes*
- *mentally or physically sick*
- *in prison.*

2 What does society as a whole do for the people on your list? Do we as a nation look after them in any way? As individuals, can we do anything to help such people? How would we go about this?

3 Should we do what we think is right because we fear the consequences if we don't?

RULES

TEACHING NOTES

The pupils' book theme

The formulation of rules is a necessary feature of human life. A large number of activities in both the personal and collective life of humans cannot proceed with any degree of order or cohesion without the regulation and guidance which rules provide. An appeal to sets of beliefs and values is an essential ingredient in the processes by which many of our more significant sets of rules are formulated, re-assessed and applied to particular situations.

The topics selected for exploration in this theme focus attention on the ways in which sets of rules need to be interpreted and applied and how they may need to be reformulated to reflect changing circumstances, knowledge, values and aspirations. An examination of rules which people believe are valid for all time, people and situations is a feature of the third topic. This theme also provides an opportunity for pupils to reflect on different attitudes to those who break rules and laws.

By this stage in their lives, most young people will be aware of the importance of rules and of the ways in which some rules reflect various beliefs, values and commitments. Many of our pupils will also be experiencing times when they wish to challenge the value and authority of certain sets of rules which impinge on their lives. Such challenges may simply be expressions of their own personal insecurity or natural antipathy towards authority. However, they may also arise from experiences in which they perceived themselves to be victims of irrational, antiquated or unjust rules. They are also likely to experience occasions when rules were strictly and rigidly applied in ways which lacked any sensitivity to the particularities of a given situation.

Pupils may also be aware that there are large numbers of people who do not accept, let alone keep, some of the rules which they tend to take for granted or are required by others to obey. Sometimes such an awareness can be very unsettling and provide yet another stimulus for questioning the value and authority of particular rules. Hence, work done in this theme should also help students reflect on ways in which some rules may be relative to particular groups and activities, while others may have a more universal value and application.

The first topic introduces pupils to some of these issues whilst the second topic is designed to heighten awareness of the ways in which people seek to make a distinction between the letter and the spirit of the law. This raises questions about authority in the context of interpreting and applying certain rules and laws. Understanding this distinction is particularly important when considering the significance of religious and moral laws, rules and codes in people's lives.

The third topic poses difficult and sensitive questions about 'relativism' and 'absolutism' in regard to religious and moral rules. It also provides an opportunity to help pupils understand ideas about how religious laws and rules may reflect past historical and cultural circumstances as well as deep spiritual insights which may transcend particular places, times and cultures.

The fourth topic of this theme is designed to help pupils reflect on a range of different attitudes towards 'rule breakers'. The focus of this topic is on exploring the relationship between particular attitudes and actions which people advocate towards those who break particular laws or rules, and the sets of beliefs and values which these attitudes and actions reflect. This, we feel, enables both teacher and pupil to get at the heart of what RE is all about.

The Activity sheets

1 This is a gentle introduction to the notion of rules. As always, the aim is to bring out the beliefs and values that underlie rules. Thinking about how they may apply in particular circumstances helps to do this. A very lively discussion can ensue if you are prepared to analyse your own school's rules as well!

2 The story of Guru Nanak's initiation is one example of someone deciding that the spirit of the law is more important than the letter of the law. In all religious traditions, the attempt to interpret rules is dogged by this problem. Often a split emerges between groups who stick to the letter of the law no matter how absurd this may seem to others, and those who try to find the essence of the law and reinterpret it for modern circumstances. This can be clearly seen in the example of the Jewish laws about the Sabbath, for example.

3 This activity sheet on the beliefs behind, and authority for, rules can be tackled as a class exercise, especially with younger or less able groups, as it requires some abstractions to be made.

4 The Ten Commandments are an interesting topic as an acceptance of them is often taken for

granted in a nominally Christian country. It is a helpful way of looking at several aspects of rules: the spirit and the letter of the law, the way in which rules are embedded in their time but can transcend it, and the possibility of different interpretations of the same rule. In a class situation, questions 1 and 2 could be done individually, and 3 and 4 discussed in groups followed by a plenary session.

5 A detailed explanation of the rules of *kashrut* is provided as a basis for a general look at the way in which keeping rules has practical consequences for the choices one can make in life, not all of which may be pleasant. A distinction is made between rules we keep because we can see a personal benefit from them (dieting to keep fit is a good example) and those that are kept because of the authority behind them.

6 It is difficult to write about Hinduism in terms of laws, as Hindu practice is extremely varied and does not rely on a canon on the same way as Christian, Muslim and Jewish practice does. However, the pattern of four aims is one that influences Hindu thinking and behaviour. Here, students translate this into everyday terms in a way which should encourage understanding of the general principle as well as reinforcing the idea that one rule can override another. Comparison can be made with Jesus's selection of the two commandments (Mark 12: 30-10) mentioned in the pupils' book.

7 This activity sheet will work best as a class exercise with a strict time limit on discussion of each example. It can be be done by dividing the class into four groups and giving each group two of the examples to discuss for five minutes on each. They then report back to the whole class on the rules they think might apply in each situation. Briefly note the authorities behind the rules as they come up, perhaps writing them on the blackboard. Time should be left for an adequate discussion of punishments: this can be done in the original groups for ten minutes, with a report-back session. The aim is to raise issues about the relationship of crimes to authorities, and of punishment (or forgiveness) to both, as a

background to looking at the religious responses to rule-breaking.

8 The broad division between the Judaeo/ Christian/Muslim religions and the Eastern ones in thinking about existence has already been noted. This naturally extends to their attitude to the idea of right and wrong actions and rewards and punishments for them. The sheet condenses the views held by the two broad types of faith, and asks the students to think about which religions are more likely to agree with each statement. It would be useful to have some examples of descriptions from a range of faiths to hand.

Christian ideas can be found in the Revelation of John in the New Testament and in Matthew 8:12, 13:42,50, 22:13, 24:51, 25:30.

Muslim descriptions can be found in the Qur'an as follows:
Paradise: Sura 9:72, 13:35, 15: 45-8, 47:15
Hell: Sura 2:175, 14:17, 25:14, 38:58-9, 76:5, 78:25, 88:7-8

There is no specific Jewish tradition about heaven and hell, although ideas fall generally into category 1.

Hindu ideas can be seen in the Bhagavad Gita 16: 1-24. The *Tao Te Ching* of Lao Tzu, although not strictly Buddhist, has some poetic passages describing the category 2 thinking; Zen Buddhist stories are also useful. Unfortunately, *nirvana* and *moksha* are often described in terms of their indescribability!

9 Forgiveness, loving one's enemies and doing good to those that hate you are Christian ideals, and forgiveness as a response to those who fall short of ideal behaviour in some circumstances is also advocated by other religions. But how does this relate to responsibility for one's actions and punishment for rule-breaking? This activity sheet can be undertaken in small-group or class discussion, or individually after some general discussion of the issues. Focussing on specific instances of rule-breaking, it raises the question of whether forgiveness is possible in all circumstances. (The fourth situation can obviously be applied to the Holocaust, Jewish responses to which are discussed in *Jews 4* in the Westhill Project series.)

What's behind the rules?

 1 *Read the passage below, which is taken from a school prospectus and describes the rules for children attending the school.*

> The school maxim is:
>
> - We work
> - We play
> - We share
> - We care
>
> The school maxim, together with high expectations, is the key to good behaviour in school. We aim to provide a disciplined, but very caring environment in which every child can feel secure. Sanctions* will have to be imposed occasionally against a child who knows and understands the school expectation but does not respect it. Corporal punishment is inappropriate and will not be used. The suspension of a child from school will be in accordance with the arrangement laid down by the Authority and the parents involved will have the right to make representation to school governors.
>
> Handbook for Alverstoke County Infant School, Gosport, Hampshire
>
> * sanctions = punishments (but not beating of any kind)

2 *Discuss (or write about) how the school above might deal with some of the following problems. Think about the general rules set out above. What sorts of punishments might be given to children who did not come up to expectations?*

a) *How would teachers deal with children who wanted to play marbles when it was time to do maths?*

b) *What would happen if a child left her lunch box at home and hadn't any food at lunchtime?*

c) *Would a disabled child be welcome in this school?*

d) *What would happen if someone was bullying others in the playground?*

e) *If a child continued to be naughty over a long period, how would you imagine the school would deal with him or her?*

Living Questions Teacher's Resource Book © 1993 Sue Hasted, Geoff Teece

The letter and the spirit of the law

In this Sikh story of Guru Nanak's youth, we can see him deciding that the spirit of the law was more important than the letter of the law.

GURU NANAK AND THE SACRED THREAD

Nanak was brought up in a good Hindu home. When he was nine years old, the priest came to put the *janeu* or sacred thread on him. It was a custom that had been handed down for thousands of years, and the priest, who was a kindly and learned man, told Nanak all about it.

'It is an ancient custom,' he said. 'Only people from the higher castes may wear the sacred thread. But you must wear it: it's the rule. Otherwise you will not go to heaven.'

Nanak thought about this. 'But anyone could wear this thread. What is to stop robbers or murderers from wearing it? And it could break, or get lost - and even when I'm wearing it, it could get dirty or get burned. No - it must be more important to be good and kind, to control evil thoughts and speak the truth than to wear a thread. Those are the rules that will make us better people, so that we can go to heaven.'

Q

1   Find out about the janeu or sacred thread. What does it mean for Hindus? Write a few words about it here:

_____

_____

_____

_____

_____

2   In your own words, say why you think Nanak decided that the spirit of the law was more important than the letter of the law.

_____

_____

_____

_____

_____

3   Can you think of any modern examples of rules where we follow the letter of the law, but not the spirit of the law?

Rules, beliefs and authority

Behind all rules are beliefs about values or standards of behaviour.

 1 *What beliefs lie behind the following rules? Write them in the space to the right of each rule. Remember, there could be more than one belief behind each rule!*

Rules	Beliefs
a) Safety belts in cars should be worn at all times when the vehicle is in motion.	
b) Illegal drugs should never be sold, bought or consumed.	
c) No smoking on the London Underground.	
d) Never swear using the name of God.	
e) Always be kind to animals.	
f) Do unto others as you would want them to do unto you.	
g) You are not to watch more than two hours' TV each day.	
h) Dress neatly and modestly in all circumstances.	
i) Equal work will be rewarded by equal pay.	
j) Children should be seen and not heard.	

2 *Now go through the rules and decide what the authority behind each one might be. Again, there could be more than one authority for each rule.*

 Living Questions Teacher's Resource Book © 1993 Sue Hasted, Geoff Teece

The Ten Commandments

 **1** *Read the following passage from the Bible. It details the commandments which the prophet Moses is said to have received from God on Mount Sinai.*

THE TEN COMMANDMENTS

God spoke, and these were his words:
"I am the Lord your God who brought you out of Egypt, where you were slaves.
"Worship no god but me.
"Do not make for yourselves images of anything in heaven or on earth or in the water under the earth. Do not bow down to any idol or worship it, because I am the Lord your God and I tolerate no rivals. I bring punishment on those who hate me and on their descendants down to the third and fourth generations. But I show my love to thousands of generations of those who love me and obey my laws.
"Do not use my name for evil purposes, for I, the Lord your God, will punish anyone who misuses my name.
"Observe the Sabbath and keep it holy. You have six days in which to do your work, but the seventh day is a day of rest dedicated to me. On that day no one is to work - neither you, your children, your slaves, your animals, nor the foreigners who live in your country. In six days I, the Lord, made the earth, the sky, the sea, and everything in them, but on the seventh day I rested. That is why I, the Lord, blessed the Sabbath and made it holy.
"Respect your father and your mother, so that you may life a long time in the land that I am giving you.
"Do not commit murder.
"Do not commit adultery.
"Do not steal.
"Do not accuse anyone falsely.
"Do not desire another man's house; do not desire his wife, his slaves, his cattle, his donkeys, or anything else that he owns."

Exodus 20: 1-17

2 *Underline in red any words or phrases in the commandments which relate to the way of life at the time when Exodus was written, for instance, references to slaves, etc.*

3 *In the pupils' book we saw how the sixth commandment about murder could be interpreted differently by people in certain situations. Can you see any other commandments which are open to more than one interpretation? If so, write down some different ways in which people understand them.*

_____

_____

_____

_____

_____

4 *Which of the commandments do many people (Christian or non-Christian) break? Which do many people keep?*

Kashrut

The laws about what Jews may eat, and not eat, are based on the book of Leviticus in the Torah. The laws are called *kashrut* and the foods which are considered fit for Jews to eat are called *kasher* foods.

Jewish people who keep these laws do so not because they are about health or hygiene, but because they believe that they are commandments from God. Not all Jews keep strict *kasher* - Orthodox Jews do, but many Reform Jews think these rules are less important than some of the other commandments, and may not keep them at all.

There are three main groups of laws:

Kasher foods

The first group of rules is about those foods that are *kasher*. They are:
- all plants, fruits and vegetables
- mammals with split hooves and which chew the cud
- fish with both scales and fins
- all domestic birds
- the milk of any *kasher* mammal
- the eggs of any *kasher* bird.

Ritual slaughter (*shehitah*)

The second group of rules is about the killing of animals for food. The rules themselves are based on the belief that slaughter must take place in the most humane way, causing the animal the least possible pain and distress. It must be done by a trained butcher (*shohet*) who understands animal anatomy and Jewish law. All blood must be drained from meat before it is eaten, because the belief is that the spirit of life is contained in the blood.

Meat and milk

The third group of rules restrict the ways in which meat and milk are used.
- Meat and milk must not be cooked together
- Meat products and milk products must not be eaten together
- Meat and milk products must not be used together.

In many Jewish homes, separate sets of cooking and eating utensils are kept to be used for the two kinds of food.

1 *In what ways do you think keeping to these rules would affect Jewish people's lives?*

2 *Are there any other rules you can think of that people keep because they come from a particular authority (such as God) rather than because of the good the rules might do them?*

Living Questions Teacher's Resource Book © 1993 Sue Hasted, Geoff Teece

Which rules are the most important?

Hindus often learn about the right way to behave from their family, and particularly from their mother.

In the Hindu tradition, a person has four aims in this life.

Although these aims are not laws in the same sense as the Ten Commandments, they do offer Hindus a way of thinking about the choices that they have in life.

THE FOUR AIMS

The first aim is pleasure, or the satisfaction of desires.

The second aim is the gaining of worldly wealth and power in order to live a prosperous adult life.

The third aim is the fulfilment of ones duties. The actual duties vary according to one's caste, stage of life, and so on.

The fourth aim is *moksha* or liberation from the endless cycle of birth and death. For most Hindus this is something only for those who are prepared to reject all worldly things; a small number of people in any one generation.

The first aim is less important than the second, and the second is less important than the third. So, whenever someone has to decide what to do, they can hold these aims in mind to help them decide what is the ideal course of action.

Q

1 Read through the first three aims again.

2 Imagine that these aims applied to everyone's life in Britain today. Can you think of three activities that might be included in each of them? Write them down in the chart below:

	Aim 1	Aim 2	Aim 3
1			
2			
3			

3 Can you think of any activities that come under aim 1 (pleasure) that you might have to give up because aim 2 (gaining prosperity) was more important? Are there any from aims 1 and 2 that might be overridden by aim 3 (duty)?

_____

_____

_____

Punishments and penalties

1 Read the following 'crime' stories.

> **a)** A young boy of 12 steals a pen from a classmate.
>
> **b)** A girl of 13 'tells' on her friends, who have been missing school to go to a daytime dance club.
>
> **c)** A young man of 16 consistently disobeys his parents, who have asked him to be home by 10.00 p.m.
>
> **d)** A man viciously kicks a dog which is tied to a lamp-post outside a supermarket.
>
> **e)** During a robbery of a post office, the postmistress is shot in the arm by the robber.
>
> **f)** A woman who has been beaten many times by her husband finally loses her temper and hits him over the head. He dies.
>
> **g)** A man poisons his wife so he is free to marry another woman.
>
> **h)** People, by their over-consumption of raw materials and energy, endanger the survival of the planet.

2 Write down any rules you think might apply in these situations.

3 What are the beliefs behind the rules? By what authority would the people be called 'criminals'?

4 What punishments, if any, do you think would be appropriate in each case? Why?

   Living Questions Teacher's Resource Book © 1993 Sue Hasted, Geoff Teece

Heaven and hell

Ideas about reward or punishment for what we have chosen to do with our lives are closely bound up with the ideas people have about time. There are two main ideas:

a)   Some people think of time as an arrow with the future ahead, the present now and the past behind us. Such people, if they believe in rewards and punishments, will tend to think of them as happening later in time, either immediately after our deaths, or on a Day of Judgement when all people who have ever lived will awaken. Some believe that this resurrection will be physical and include our bodies; others think of it as a spiritual event, and of our spirits or souls as separate from our bodies, which will have died and decayed.

They may also think of the reward and punishment as 'heaven' and 'hell', places to which we will be sent as we deserve. Heaven is often described in terms of pleasant experiences such as being in a garden, meeting old and loved friends or angels and good spirits, and being close to God. Hell is described as its opposite, sometimes with the Devil or demons inflicting torture on 'the damned' or burning them in an eternal fire.

b)   Other people think of time as a continuous present in which 'past' and 'future' are illusions. People who think of eternity as 'the eternal now' are more likely to think of the reward for right actions as a kind of awakening to the presence of God. In fact, they would say, God is always present here and now and in everything, but our attachment to the many illusions of our daily lives blinds us to his presence.

Such people will tend to see the 'punishment' for wrong action as a continuing immersion in the pain, worry and distress caused by being caught up in illusion. Some people who think like this may also say that, although individual human lives end in death, our consciousness is reborn again and again until we escape illusion and awake to awareness.

 1   Which world religions do you think would broadly agree with each point of view?

2   If you can, find some examples of descriptions of heaven and hell, and some of nirvana or moksha.

Forgiveness

Forgiveness is an ideal held up by people of all faiths. However, it is not always seen as the most important ideal.

Q *1 Four situations are described below. Read each one and think about it. Then say whether you would find it possible to forgive the offence in each of them. Give the reasons for your decision.*

a Your best friend has stolen your boyfriend/girlfriend. You introduced them to each other, and made a point of telling each of them how much you valued the other.

b Your house has been ransacked and your most prized possession stolen. When the police catch the thieves, it emerges that the main offender is a young man your own age who has a troubled history. He has no family, no place to live and owns very little himself.

c Your little sister is run over and killed by a drunken driver. He did not do it deliberately and is terribly sorry for what has happened.

d You are the sole survivor of a massacre in which your whole family was deliberately killed by people who were quite sane but believed you deserved to die. When these people are brought to justice, you meet them. They express no regrets for what they have done.

Living Questions Teacher's Resource Book © 1993 Sue Hasted, Geoff Teece

SUFFERING

TEACHING NOTES

The pupils' book theme

Suffering in one form or another touches everyone. It can come in spasmodic waves or it can be a chronic condition. It can be accepted as an inevitable consequence of natural processes and life events or it can be rejected as an unnecessary and pointless result of human ignorance, failure, neglect or aggression.

The topics used to develop this theme highlight some of the positive and perhaps creative responses to human suffering.

The first two topics focus on the different ways in which suffering seems to be an inevitable and necessary part of the natural order. Attention is drawn to various features of the food chain in which the survival of a large number of species depends on the use of other species for food. In such cases, apparent suffering is the means by which life goes on and nature seeks to maintain a viable balance between the species. Pupils are also helped to identify the role of pain in warning the body of possible greater harm. Pain as a symptom of disease and injury also plays an important role in maintaining human health and well being. The place of pain in human childbirth is explored along with religious ideas about the idea of spiritual progress as a kind of 'rebirth'. The Buddhist idea that suffering is an inevitable part of being alive is explored in the final section of this topic.

The third topic opens up opportunities for pupils to describe and classify a number of ways in which people use pain and suffering as a means of achieving certain goals, some of which are religious. The use of pain or at least strict controls and disciplines to increase physical strength, extend endurance levels and push back pain thresholds, is a common factor in many great human achievements and some examples are explored in the first section. Within the religious field attention is given to the use of various forms of ascetic behaviour to heighten spiritual awareness, deepen commitment and stimulate compassion for other suffering people. Examples of self-sacrifice on behalf of others also abound in religious traditions. For Christians, the example of Jesus reveals this positive use of suffering for the salvation of the world.

In the fourth topic the focus shifts away from the nature and causes of suffering and on to the ways in which people cope with suffering. Pupils are encouraged to gather information about various community efforts, activities and programmes designed to remove or lessen the amount of suffering in human experience. Educational and advertising campaigns designed to improve health and safety can be analysed as responses to suffering. In the same way, looking at the range of welfare and charity programmes offered by governments, religious and other community groups from this perspective can also assist the pupils in their reflection on the challenges presented by suffering.

These examples of communal responses to suffering are paralleled in the text with examples of more personal ways of coping with suffering. Other examples of people who use such spiritual means as prayer, meditation, yoga and solitude as a way of coping with both personal and collective suffering can also be studied as an important feature of this topic. The topic ends with an example which is intended as a challenge to pupils' ideas about what constitutes suffering.

The Activity sheets

1 'Suffering' is a very broad term. This activity sheet offers a way of preparing for work on the topic at home, by watching TV. Thinking about what can be done for sufferers by others, or by themselves, prepares the ground for categorising responses to suffering. A very few examples of suffering connected with beliefs may arise; it is also possible to discuss the beliefs of those who respond to suffering in a review session.

2 Another activity sheet to do early in the topic, this can be done as a whole class exercise or in small groups, with the central section providing a chance for individual reflection. The suffering that is apparent in the natural order raises problems for many people: how does it square with the idea of a loving God, for example? The death of relations or pet animals may come up in discussion, and obviously, sensitivity is required in relating the particular to the general.

3 Siddhartha is, of course, Buddha. Buddhism can be seen as having developed from this young man's meditation on the suffering that is an inevitable part of being human. Many young people (and quite a few old ones) see every illness and death, at whatever age, as tragedy, and think of happiness as inseparable from youth (and at least a little wealth!). It is worth exploring why the Buddha rejected this way of seeing things.

4 The topic makes the point that pain and suffering can be used in different ways, and

sheets 4, 5 and 6 explore aspects of this idea. This one examines the aims that people are prepared to suffer for, and tries to bring out the values behind them. What goal is so important that we are prepared to suffer for it?

5 Suffering can also be used as a way of raising awareness, as this story shows. In real life, the guests at the fund-raising dinner shared the food between them so that all had an equally delicious meal and none went hungry. The idea was to demonstrate the relationship of the 'developed' and 'developing' nations in a concrete way. In moving from this to Ramadan, it should be emphasised that fasting to raise awareness of hunger is only one aspect of many for Muslims. Alms-giving (*zakat*) is one of the consequences. Other practices that could be mentioned in this context include meditation and yoga, both of which use sensory deprivation or control to heighten awareness.

6 It has to be recognised that there are many apparently negative uses of pain and suffering, too. Looking at why these come about and exploring the underlying values can, however, be very instructive. Some religious examples (e.g. self-flagellation by Christians or Muslims) may come up in discussion. Sometimes a practice that may appear repulsive or distasteful to observers may have an aim that they can recognise, even if they do not share it, and this can lead to dialogue and understanding.

7 The final three activity sheets cover responses to suffering. This one, although presented as an individual task, can be done as a class exercise with hexagons made from sugar paper and stuck as a patchwork onto a display board. The colours can be varied to divide the different fields of human activity. Here we are talking about community and public or social responses to suffering. Those which have a religious basis need to be highlighted in some way, perhaps by adding a gold sticky star to the hexagons concerned.

8 The story of Terry Waite shows a personal response to suffering with a strong Christian base. The emphasis in this sheet is on personal responses to one's own suffering. Students can be encouraged to find examples among people they know, as well as among the more famous. The 'children of courage' to whom awards are presented each year can provide some examples. The idea that suffering can serve to deepen one's commitment to a cause or faith can be brought out through examples of, for instance, hunger strikers or pacifists imprisoned for their beliefs.

9 The Book of Job as a whole is too long for reading aloud in class, but it would be worth reading a small section to give the feel of this poetic Jewish exploration of the question of suffering; even in English, the language is beautiful. The condensed version given here serves its purpose of raising questions, but robs the story of its original power. Working out questions to ask on Job's behalf is a way of summing up the thinking students have done on the topic. Students may then like to find some English poems which deal with suffering, and share them or make their own small anthology to reflect their view of the subject.

TV survey

Suffering is widespread and takes many forms. One way of finding out about the extent of suffering is to do a TV survey.

Choose three programmes to watch: one should be a soap opera, one the news, and one other of your choice.

Q *1 In the left-hand column in the chart below, write down in note form all the examples of suffering you see or hear about in each programme. Do this while you are watching - your notes can be brief, e.g. 'bomb victims ', 'mourners' and so on. You will probably need more paper.*

2 Afterwards, in the right-hand column write down anything that can be done about each example of suffering, and who would do it. For instance, bomb victims might be treated in hospital by nurses and doctors, and mourners might be comforted by their family and representatives of their faith. Those who suffer can also do things for themselves; note these, too.

Use a separate sheet if you need more room.

Examples of suffering	What could be done?

3 Are there any examples here of people whose beliefs affect their suffering in any way? Underline the examples if so.

Is suffering part of the natural order of things?

Q **1** In a small group, brainstorm as many examples of things that cause suffering as you can in five minutes. Write them down here.

_____

_____

_____

_____

_____

_____

_____

_____

2 On your own, underline any of them that seem to be part of the natural order of things, that are inevitable in some way. Choose three of them and write them each in turn in the left-hand column below. In the right-hand column, write down why you think your chosen examples of suffering are simply a part of existence.

3 In your group again, discuss where you think suffering comes from. Is it inevitable for human beings? Is there ever a purpose to suffering? How does the fact of suffering relate to ideas about God? Note down any questions you have, or any conclusions you reach, in the space below.

_____

_____

_____

_____

_____

    Living Questions Teacher's Resource Book © 1993 Sue Hasted, Geoff Teece

Prince Siddhartha's encounter with suffering

In about 563 BCE, a prince was born into the royal Gautama family of the tribe of Shakya in north-east India, in a town called Lumbini which is now in Nepal. Before he was born, his mother had strange dreams which indicated that he would be special, and soon afterwards the wise men told his father that his new son would grow up to be an emperor or a great religious teacher.

The king did not want his son to become a religious teacher, because that would mean his leaving his family and kingdom and choosing a hard, solitary life of meditation wandering in the forest. So he tried to make Siddhartha's life as happy as possible, in the hope that he would never start questioning the meaning of life. Siddhartha grew up surrounded by beautiful things in the palace and its gardens. He married a princess and they had a son.

Eventually Siddhartha grew bored and wanted to explore outside the palace and its environs. He asked a servant to drive him out to the villages in his chariot. There he saw three things he had never been allowed to see before: an old man, a sick man, and a dead man. When he asked his charioteer whether he could ever be old or sick or die, the charioteer told him he could and would. He was shocked. Then they saw a fourth man who was wandering and meditating on the suffering and impermanence of life, and Siddhartha knew what he had to do.

He went home. One night when his wife and son were asleep, he took a sword and cut off his long black hair, and left the palace, taking none of his rich possessions with him. In this way he began the journeys which would lead in time to his enlightenment.

 1 *Can you guess who this story is about? What was his name after his enlightenment, and what does it mean?*

2 *The happiness that Siddhartha knew in the palace was based on being young and healthy and having many possessions. Why do you think he rejected this happiness?*

What are you prepared to suffer for?

People are often prepared to 'suffer' for
things that they think are important or aims
that they want to achieve.

 1   See if you can find at least three examples of this kind of suffering in some of the following fields of human endeavour:

the arts   medicine   science   politics   exploration
          sport   childcare   teaching   religion

They do not have to be examples about famous people. And remember, 'suffering' in this sense includes self control, discipline and endurance and may not mean actual physical pain. To 'suffer' means to 'allow'.

2   Put your chosen examples on the left.
In the second column, describe the goal or aim of the person or people concerned.
In the third column, write down what kind of suffering they were prepared to undergo in order to achieve that goal. (We have done one example to start you off.)

Example	Aim or goal	What they were prepared to suffer
Liz McColghan (Sport)	Win Olympic Gold medal for running.	Hard training twice a day. Limited time with family. Strict diet.

3   What beliefs and values are important enough to people for them to be prepared to suffer for them? Look at your second column aims or goals. What values do they represent? Write down some examples of such values, if you can.

          Living Questions Teacher's Resource Book © 1993 Sue Hasted, Geoff Teece

Using suffering

Have you ever felt really hungry? Do you know what it feels like to be hungry when there is no food to be had?

Sometimes, heightening our awareness of such things can give us a new insight into what it is like to be someone else, someone who, perhaps, is suffering in ways we could not imagine.

Feeling hungry?

A charity concerned with aid for the hungry held a fund-raising dinner. Everyone who wanted to go paid the same sum for a ticket - most of the money would go to help the charity. When the tickets came, a few were pink and the rest, the great majority, were white.

When they got to the place where the dinner was to be held, the ticket holders were surprised to see one small table at the head of the room on a platform, laden down with meat and salads and fruit and cream cakes, and many larger tables on the lower floor, with one large communal bowl of rice and some pieces of dry bread on each. Those with the pink tickets were ushered up to the top table with the feast upon it, and those with the white ones were packed off to the tables with the rice. At the top table there were waiters to serve the drinks; at the lower tables, there was only water, and people had to help themselves.

The guests all felt very awkward. Those at the top table were embarrassed - how could they tuck in to this delicious food while the others, who had so little, were all watching them? Those at the lower tables couldn't help being angry. After all, they had paid the same sum for their ticket - why shouldn't they have nice food, too, instead of plain rice?

Eventually the organisers pointed out that this was exactly the situation in the world today, with a few rich countries enjoying plenty, while most of the world's people have very little.

 1 **What do you think happened next? Write a short paragraph to end the story, saying what you imagine the guests did, and why. Had they learned anything from their suffering?**

2 **One of the reasons that Muslims fast during the month of Ramadan is to stimulate their compassion for those who are poor and hungry. Find out about Ramadan. Can you find some ways in which Muslims show their compassion for the needy and suffering?**

Violence

Much suffering and pain in the world result from violence of various kinds.
What makes people violent towards each other?

 1 Make a list of all the negative examples of pain and suffering you can think of in the space below.

2 Now discuss the following situations. In particular, try to think about these two questions:
a) What do people who are violent think they can achieve by being violent?
b) What values and beliefs lie behind the violence in each one?

Domestic   At the personal level, there is domestic violence. Women or children, and sometimes men, can be badly hurt or even killed when relationships go wrong. What causes this kind of violence? Where do you draw the line between parental punishment of children who are naughty, and violence?

Criminal   Crime often involves violence, pain and suffering. What makes people get involved in robbery or blackmail? What do they think they can achieve that way? What do they think about their victims?

Military   When we go to war, we know that people will suffer. For what sorts of reasons do nations go to war? How do we justify this to ourselves? Is it right to see other human beings as enemies?

Political   Acts of terrorism, hijacking, kidnapping, persecution, torture and murder are sometimes carried out in the name of a political goal, such as the establishment of a new nation or a political belief. Does the end justify the means?

   Living Questions Teacher's Resource Book © 1993 Sue Hasted, Geoff Teece

Responses to suffering

Q *1   Much social effort goes towards the relief of suffering. See if you can complete the patchwork below by filling it with examples of groups or individual people, religious or non-religious, who work to relieve suffering.*

To help you, you could think about some of the following areas of activity:

Science   Technology   Publishing
Housing   Education   Media (TV, newspapers, books)
Social Services   Overseas aid   Religion (faith communities)
Medicine/health care

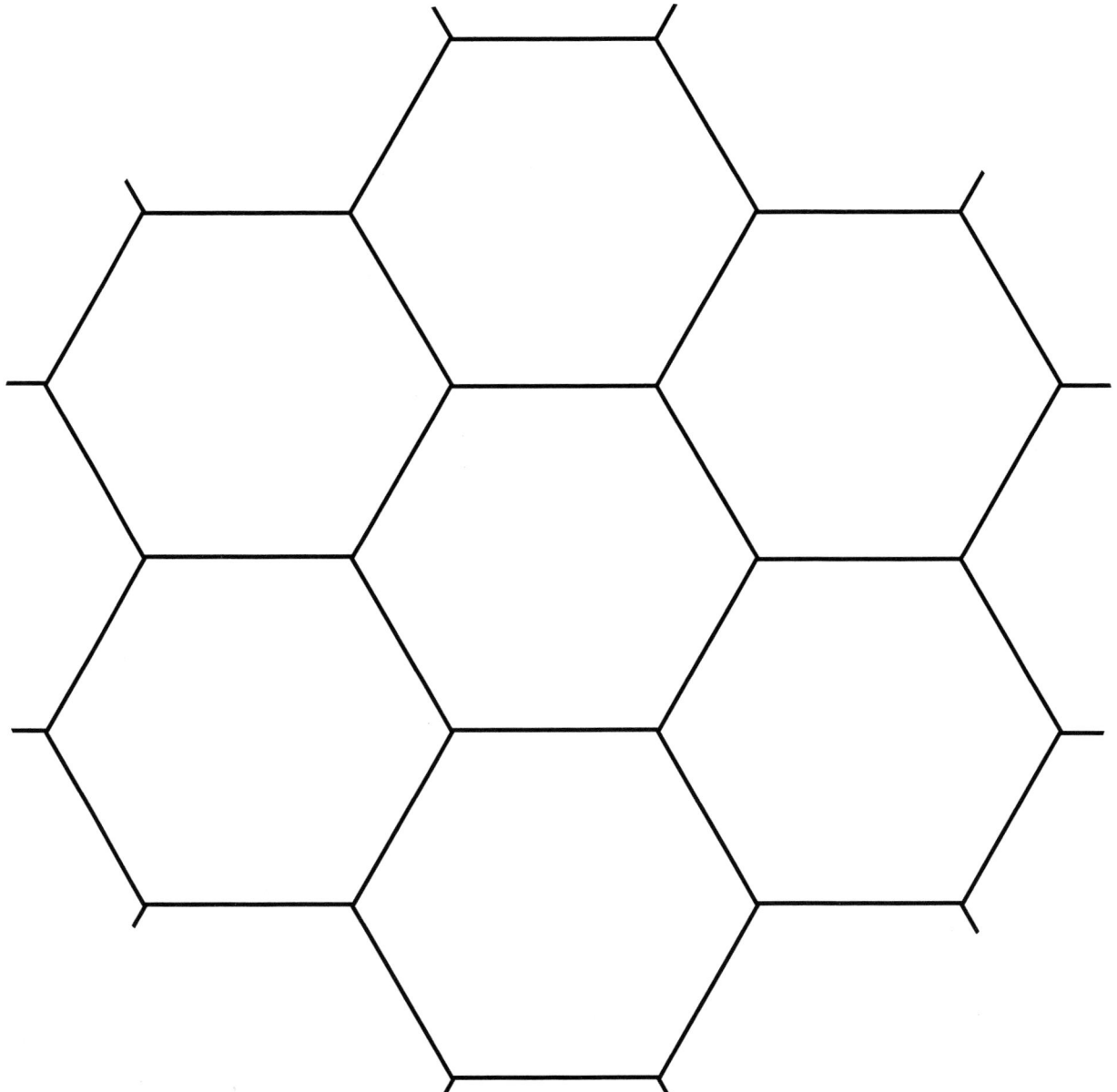

2   Why do we want to help others who suffer? In a small group, discuss this statement for five minutes:

'It is a natural human response to want to help those who are suffering.'

Personal responses to suffering

Terry Waite, a Christian, was working as the Archbishop of Canterbury's envoy (messenger) when he was kidnapped in Beirut, Lebanon, in 1987. At the time he was trying to help bring about the release of several other hostages who had been kidnapped previously.

Terry was held prisoner for four years. He was tortured with beatings and a mock execution. In an interview after his release he said:

'Somehow I found that it was possible to go a certain distance within myself, to sort of step back and almost step outside myself and see myself in That position being threatened with immediate death. That was quite extraordinary, but my faith came to my aid.

The remarkable thing about faith is that it's not a sudden flash from Heaven [...], it's just something that quietly sustains. I would say to myself "You can do your worst but you can't destroy me. Never." They didn't.'

Terry also said that he sympathised with his Lebanese captors' own suffering, and understood why they had taken him hostage, although he couldn't sympathise with the means they had chosen to achieve their ends.

'It has been a deepening experience. It has been something which I will be able to utilise for the sake of other suffering people. I'm conscious of the people who suffer greatly in the Middle East. I have every sympathy for their suffering.

I am conscious of the people who suffer in Northern Ireland. I am conscious of the people who were used as human shields in Iraq and I shall be able to do something, I hope, to assist all these suffering groups of people to understand their suffering and convert it into something that is creative.'

Q 1 Does Terry tell us anything about what he sees as the source of his courage and capacity to endure his long captivity? Do you think his suffering deepened his commitment to his faith? What does he hope to do with his experience?

2 What other personal responses to suffering do you know of? Find some examples of things that people do to cope with their own suffering (not other people's), and note them down. Underline any that have a religious belief as a basis.

 Living Questions Teacher's Resource Book © 1993 Sue Hasted, Geoff Teece

The story of Job

The following story is condensed from the Book of Job in the Bible. Some people see this beautiful poem as a collection of Jewish answers to the question 'What is suffering?'

Job lived in the land of Uz. He was a good man who worshipped God and was careful not to do evil. One day Satan (the devil) appeared before God and taunted God, saying that Job was only good because God had always protected him. 'If you took away everything he has, he'd curse you!' said Satan. God agreed to let Satan put Job to the test, as long as he did not hurt him.

Poor Job! First, his servants, who were out ploughing his fields, were killed and his donkeys stolen. Next lightning struck Job's shepherds and sheep and killed them. Then raiders attacked and stole his camels, killing those who guarded them. Finally a desert wind blew down the house of Job's eldest son, killing all his children, who had gone there for a feast.

Job tore his clothes in grief and started to mourn. 'I was born with nothing,' he said, 'and I will die with nothing. The Lord gave, and now he has taken away. May his name be praised.'

Satan was disappointed that Job had not cursed God as he had predicted. He said that this was only because Job wanted to stay alive. 'If you hurt his body, he will curse you,' he said. God let Satan test Job further, as long as he did not kill him.

Satan made terrible sores break out all over Job's body. Job's wife asked him why he did not curse God for all his misfortunes, but Job replied 'When God sends us something good, we welcome it. How can we complain when he sends us trouble?'

Three friends came to comfort Job, and sat in silence with him as he suffered. Job cursed the day he was born, but still refused to curse God. Eventually the friends said that Job must have done something bad to merit this punishment, but Job protested his innocence. However, he did begin to question why God was treating him in this way.

God's answer was unexpected. It was that Job could not expect to understand the workings of the Creator. Immediately, Job apologised for speaking out of turn: 'I knew of you then only by report, but now I see you with my own eyes.'

God then restored Job's fortunes, and he went on to live to a great old age, and had many more children.

Q *1 Read the story of Job. Then try to write down some of the questions about the causes of suffering Job might have wanted to ask.*